TopGear
DRIVES OF A LIFETIME

AROUND THE WORLD IN

25
ROAD TRIPS

1 3 5 7 9 10 8 6 4 2

BBC Books, an imprint of Ebury Publishing
20 Vauxhall Bridge Road,
London SW1V 2SA

BBC Books is part of the Penguin Random House group of companies whose
addresses can be found at global.penguinrandomhouse.com

Text © Top Gear 2015

Top Gear (word marks and logos) is a trademark of the British Broadcasting
Corporation and used under licence. Top Gear © 2005

First published by BBC Books in 2015

www.eburypublishing.co.uk

A CIP catalogue record for this book is available from the British Library

ISBN 9781849909693

Commissioning editor: Lorna Russell
Project editor: Charlotte Macdonald
Design: Akihiro Nakayama and Two Associates
Maps © ML Design
All images © Top Gear

Printed and bound in China by C&C Offset Printing Co., Ltd

Penguin Random House is committed to a sustainable future for
our business, our readers and our planet. This book is made from
Forest Stewardship Council® certified paper.

CONTENTS

INTRODUCTION

If you paid attention at school, you'll know that the world has seven continents, and that penguins come from the bottom one. You'll know that the equator is a 24,901-mile belt around our planet's midriff, and that if you tunneled from one pole to another you'd have a 7,900-mile hole and a large heap of dirt to dispose of.

In other words, it's quite a big place and, over the last 20 years or so, *TopGear* has explored many of its weirder corners. We've driven at maximum speed through the Australian outback, crossed Burma in rusty trucks and driven to the world's most heavily militarised border armed with nothing but a small green hatchback.

We've driven up a volcano, during an earthquake, while it was erupting. To cool down, we went to Antarctica with some bulldozers. Deserts, mountains, jungles, frozen wastelands and the A93 just outside Braemar. We've been there, done that, and got the parking tickets.

This book is a collection of more recent adventures, documented by *TopGear* magazine's writers and photographers, with a sprinkling of adventures from the *TopGear* telly show. Each story is accompanied by a handy travel guide, including useful information such as how to get there, which route to take, and how much anti-venom to pack.

These are not the five-star trips you see in glossy brochures. Some you could do next week, others need a little more planning and a few vaccinations. But they all prove one thing: sometimes, a good road trip isn't just about the car.

Sure, everyone dreams of driving a red Ferrari into a pink sunset. But have you ever considered taking a cheap, brown 4x4 up a Peruvian canyon named after ducks? Don't rule it out.

Finally, and to help you navigate the book like a hardy explorer, we've split the world into three handy geographical sections: top, middle and bottom. We'd have been a bit more precise, if we'd paid more attention at school…

THE MOTHER ROAD

FOR AN AMBITIOUS ROAD TRIP, YOU CAN'T BEAT ROUTE 66. AND FOR AMBITIOUS CARS, YOU CAN'T BEAT A BUGATTI VEYRON. SEE WHERE THIS IS GOING?

On a packed Santa Monica Pier, sprawl of LA to the right, Pacific Ocean to the left, the pneumatic blonde – hair dyed porcelain-white, bosoms overinflated as basketballs, hot pants lacquered to posterior – leans over the Veyron's door, inch-long eyelashes almost brushing my face. 'Can I get a ride?'

'Er, no,' I reply. 'I'm not famous. I'm… English. It's not my car.'

Pneumatic Blonde's demeanour switches, flick-knife style, from coquettish to caustic. 'Then get off the frickin' pier!' And away she huffs, six-inch heels stomping the boardwalk, in hunt of a man of true wealth and, eventually, a messy, profitable divorce settlement.

And in that instant it pops, the dizzy sense of euphoria,

of utter relief, at having delivered a two-million quid, 260mph hypercar – the greatest car in the world, no question – on the biggest, daftest road trip in *TG* history, 2,404 miles from Chicago to the LA waterfront without damage, speeding ticket or the most retweeted crash in history. Seven days of heady, sun-drenched strangeness, and it ends with a verbal bitch-slap from a wannabe WAG made of 85 per cent aftermarket parts and with a cleavage running 55psi. But, hey, what great road trip doesn't?

It began, of course, at the beginning, two time zones and seven days earlier at the eastern end of Route 66, on the shore of Lake Michigan. Only it didn't, because, in true *TG*

WHERE IS IT?
The US of A

WHICH BIT?
Between Chicago and LA

GIVE ME CO-ORDINATES!
34.863465, -115.119040

WHEN SHOULD I GO?
America is open all year round, which is handy

HOW LONG WILL IT TAKE?
You can properly explore most stuff in two weeks, although we did it quicker

HOW DO I GET THERE?
Many aircraft land in the United States. Get yourself a seat aboard one

WHAT'S THE WEATHER LIKE?
A bit of everything

WHAT'S THE ROAD LIKE?
Long

WHAT IF I GET LOST?
They have maps and road signs and everything. Failing that, ask a local from a safe distance

TG TOP TIP:
Do it the correct way around, by starting in Chicaco and ending in LA on Santa Monica pier

ONE MORE THING:
Route 66 was originally supposed to be called Route 60, but that number was taken

fashion, we failed to find the official start point of Route 66: Jackson Boulevard, a block west of the Chicago waterfront. That road was closed for a skiffle festival or somesuch, so after a half-hour loop downtown and photographer Justin somehow setting the satnav language to Dutch, we figured close was good enough and picked up 66, with its tell-tale brown-shield signs, as it wound south-west out of the city, through suburbs described by estate agents as 'up and coming' and by the rest of us as 'a trifle stabby'. The weather was hot and windy and frantic, weather so annoyed it can't decide what it wants to be.

Through Joliet, home to one of America's nastiest prisons – 'DON'T STOP FOR HITCHHIKERS!' – I caught sight of a low, silvery bullet, reflected in a shop window. And then it hit like an electric shock. Bloody Hell I'm Driving A Bugatti Veyron On Route 66. As experiences go, that's not so much bucket list as just… bucket.

The Veyron. At the time of writing, the fastest car in the world, the car that crowned Captain Slow a speed-record holder, the car that redefined our grasp of fast. The car we declared, in 2013, the greatest in *TG* mag's history. And not just any Veyron, but the Veyron Grand Sport Vitesse, the convertible version of the faster version of the fastest production car in history. A brief reminder, if you needed it: 1,200bhp from an 8.0-litre quad-turbo W16, 1,100lb ft of torque, seven-speed DSG, 4WD, asking price north of two million quid. Officially the GSV will do 0–62mph in 2.5secs, the quarter-mile in 10 flat and 260mph vmax. In pub ammo stakes, that's an atom bomb.

CHICAGO

Belleville

Springfield

Tulsa

Oklahoma

Amarillo

Santa Fe

Las Vegas

Flagstaff

Riverside

LOS ANGELES

What *is* Route 66? At its simplest level, it's – and you may have guessed this one – a road. Born in 1926, it was one of America's first east–west arteries, joining Chicago and the Midwest to distant California. 66's fame, and traffic, mushroomed in the Thirties, as escapees of the Dust Bowl – the farming crisis that rendered much of the Great Plains barren, unfarmable – headed west to California in (often fruitless) search of work, a journey chronicled in John Steinbeck's *The Grapes of Wrath*.

'66 is the mother road,' wrote Steinbeck. 'The road of flight.' Thousands of refugees from Missouri, Oklahoma and Texas loaded up their jalopies and lumbered across the desert, Route 66 becoming the path, the symbol of America's Depression-era migration west. After becoming the USA's first fully paved highway in 1938, 66 enjoyed a renaissance in the fifties and sixties, as newly monied middle America developed a taste for the road trip. Route 66 became the vacation corridor to California, crackling with motels, diners and gas stations. Reduced to irrelevance in later years by modern four-lane freeways, 66 remains – in part at least – ossified in its sixties prime, a time-capsule metaphor for the freedom of America's West, and the freedom of the car. The original road trip, all 2,400 miles of it.

At vmax, the Veyron could get from Chicago to LA in just under nine hours. Sorry to disappoint, but we didn't vmax it the whole way. This is partly because *TopGear*'s fuel budget doesn't stretch to a 100-litre refill every 52 miles, but mostly because doing 260mph on a public highway is a) a trifle antisocial and b) likely to irk the law-enforcement community somewhat. On almost every highway, local sheriffs hovered like reef sharks in the central reservation, just waiting for the next unsuspecting klutz to wander a few miles an hour over the ludicrously slow speed limit.

Call it an exercise in self-restraint. There's a gauge on the dash telling you exactly how many of the GSV's available 1,200bhp you're utilising at any moment. Most of the time, we'd be employing barely 50bhp. Four per cent of the Bugatti's potential. So you get your kicks where you can find them, and in small doses. Accelerating from an on-ramp up to freeway speeds in the Veyron, I discovered, is like giving the faintest press to the world's most enormous pair of bellows. The gentlest whoosh of air, and then from 30mph to 75mph in an almost imperceptible blink. A second too long on the throttle, and you'd be looking

at a lengthy spell in the state penitentiary, and the close attentions of a mustachioed convict named Bubba.

States three and four arrived quickly: a dozen-mile wiggle through the south-eastern nubbin of Kansas, through the once-booming mining town of Galena (famed pre-Prohibition, my guidebook sagely noted, for its 'saloons and bawdy houses') and over the border into the red dirt of Oklahoma, and billboard central.

'BEEN ACCUSED OF DOMESTIC VIOLENCE?' grinned a plastic-haired, fake-tanned lawyer from an 80-foot roadside erection. 'I CAN GET YOU OFF!' You stay classy, America.

'MARRIAGE = ONE MAN + ONE WOMAN,' read another, for a church. Followed, below, by: ''CONFUSED? JUST ASK ME' – GOD.' That's right, a billboard with a *direct quote* from the Almighty.

If you've got the big man on speed-dial, guys, we could use his help sorting out the path of the One True 66. See, as we quickly discovered, 66 isn't really a road. Or at least, not one road. Since its birth in the twenties, the route underwent near-constant upgrade, with new 'alignments' arriving every decade or so. But here's the thing. The newer sections didn't always replace the older sections but simply bypassed them instead, the original track relegated to an access road, or to rot into oblivion. Much of it is still there. At any given time, pottering happily down a section of Fifties 66, on your right will be the fissured, concrete remnants of the 1926 original route, while to the left will run a newer section, each with their period array of gas stations and diners. To tackle the 'original' '26 alignment would require a) some high-grade satellite mapping and b) a mighty sturdy off-roader. For the rest of us, following 66 involves a continual skip between decades, a drive-through history of America's roads.

Which is the true Route 66? All of them. None of them. In truth, it doesn't really matter. Because Route 66 isn't really a strip of tarmac, it's a patchwork of history, interwoven and overlaid.

★ ★ ★ ★ ★

Adrian, Texas (population 149, classified as a city, go figure) declares itself Route 66's halfway point. Of course, the precise halfway point depends on which wiggles before and after you believe constitute the 'real' 66, but Adrian seems as good a spot as any. At the self-proclaimed centre (1,139 miles to Chicago, 1,139 to Los Angeles, reads the sign) stands the Midpoint diner, an immaculate slice of Fifties Americana. We stopped for waffles and French toast, and watched tumbleweed bumble its way down the highway, as the diner's owner explained how, after decades in the doldrums, 66 is picking up again, with drivers and bikers from all over the world making the pilgrimage down America's original main street.

Right on cue, a swarm of some 40 bikers – Harleys, leathers, the hum of petrol and triple-cooked sweat – parked up some 50 yards from the Veyron. Uh-oh. I've read Hunter S Thompson's *Hell's Angels*. I know about these biker gangs and the 'stompings' they dish out to any ostentatious

interlopers on their patch. And you can't interlope much more ostentatiously than with a silver convertible Veyron. Photographer Justin and I scrambled from the banquette and out to the car.

The gang's leader – a big fella, maybe six-three, wiry, dirt-brown face and skull bandana – strode over to the Bug, cracking knuckles deliberately. I did my best to look as unthreatening as possible, which, being a short, round man from England, is really quite unthreatening. As the leather-wrapped brute straightened up and shook his head gently from side to side, presumably to loosen the punching muscles, I got ready to sample the taste of Doc Martens.

'Alright, butt, where's this from?'

The leader of the biker gang turned out to be a Welsh accountant named Rhys from Caerphilly. He was tackling 66 with a bunch of other Welsh accountant mates on hired bikes, taking a month to do it, living the full American dream: sleepin' under the stars, cookin' round a log fire, rubbin' talc into saddle-sore buttocks. He offered to trade the Veyron for his battered rental Harley. We politely refused.

a huge snowplough. 'What ye really need is one of those,' he says. The plough, it turns out, is attached to the front of a PistenBully 600. For those of you unfamiliar with the world of snow grooming, the 600 is the Ferrari of piste bashers. Like our actual Ferrari, it costs a quarter of a million quid. Unlike our Ferrari, it has a 12.8-litre straight-six diesel made by Mercedes. And with 1,620lb ft of torque, it out-grunts the FF by two-and-a-half to one. Most importantly, it has a set of steel tracks that spread its 12-tonne weight over the soft snow. Last night, it combed the slopes, creating a nice smooth surface in preparation for our climb. If the crust hadn't melted, we might have made it.

No matter. While some supercars would've headed for a garage ages ago, the FF put its wellies on. People have said it's not a proper Ferrari, but while their 'proper' Ferraris keep warm at home, this one has brought me here. Parked among the battered Discoveries and Foresters in the Glenshee car park, it looks proper enough to me. Now, if someone could pass me a shovel, we'll be off...

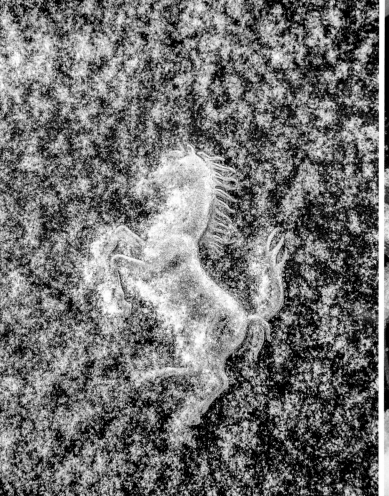

WHITE LITE

ONE BALEARIC ISLAND, ONE LIGHTWEIGHT PORSCHE, ONE VERY SHORT NIGHT. ASK YOURSELF: WHAT WOULD YOU DO?

Mallorca has blown a very big fuse. This is my first thought upon spearing out of yet another pretty-but-identikit rural village, because as soon as we leave the immediate environs, the night sky wraps around the Cayman like a black velvet shroud, turning the ice-white Porsche into a faintly glowing, unquiet ghost. Being let loose in the Cayman R, the lightened and tightened version of one of the most useful sports cars in existence, up a Mallorcan mountain road at night sounds quite cool, but believe me, at this point there's a horrible, gut-boiling sense of frustration running through me like a dirty infection. And it has nothing to do with dodgy tapas.

The fact is that there are precisely no streetlights to give even the vaguest hint as to which way the road goes. Not one. Any ambient starlight or moonglow is diffused by heavy cloud, and the road is simply too twisty to get any solid idea of direction. The wraithlike little Porsche is fitted with the excellent optional xenons, but it's still impossible to drive even vaguely quickly without risking inconvenient death. Worse, the roads are actually pretty good. But you can sense the doomy drops off the inky edges, and the corners have a nasty habit of tightening at the last moment. Like trying to run across a large room in pitch darkness, you can sense the space even if you can't see it, and you belt along cringing, awaiting the moment when you meet the scenery with your face. It's all about confidence, and I appear to have left mine at the hotel.

I can't believe this. Gifted a hardcore Porsche and a mountain range, and I can't even find a decent bloody road to drive it on.

WHERE IS IT?
On the north coast of Mallorca, the big Balearic

WHICH BIT?
From Panta de Gorg Blau to Sa Calobra

GIVE ME CO-ORDINATES!
39.829738, 2.8146

WHEN SHOULD I GO?
Pick a quiet morning outside of the tourist season when it'll feel like your own private island.

HOW LONG WILL IT TAKE?
Depends how brave you're feeling. Plan for half an hour each way

HOW DO I GET THERE?
Grab a budget flight to Palma, drive north along the main road, turn left at the lake

WHAT'S THE WEATHER LIKE?
Sticky

WHAT'S THE ROAD LIKE?
Snaky

WHAT IF I GET LOST?
It's on an island, so try smoke signals. And if that fails, the mainland is a short swim away

TG TOP TIP:
Watch out for cyclists. Believe it or not, they come here to ride up the road… for pleasure

ONE MORE THING:
The road was designed by an Italian engineer and features a spiral bridge about halfway along

Grinding the point home is the Cayman's overwhelming sense of potential. Ghosting through these orange-lit Mallorcan villages, the R potters with sublime ease, riding better than a standard Cayman S, despite being lowered a not-insignificant 20mm, failing to graunch over speed bumps, sucking lumps into the dampers like a tiny, perfect magic trick. On light throttle openings, the 330bhp 3.4 sounds, frankly, like it has a blowing exhaust, the familiar flat-six hoarseness akin to a dog coughing up an angora sweater, but on brief revels to three-quarters of the rev-range, the wail starts to build. Just as I have to slow for the next village. Frustration becomes a familiar – and infinitely bitter – taste in the back of my throat.

Eventually we stop to take pictures in a sleepy village and immediately cause a bit of a stir. It could be the sight of two men assembling a photographic rig that looks like some sort of siege engine in the middle of the street at 1am, or it could be the Cayman. A mallowy wobble of craggy old lady shuffles over to poke us with her walking stick, so I smile and point at the Porsche, miming picture-taking in some sort of bizarre late-night version of *Give Us a Clue*, becoming increasingly camp during the whole wordless exchange. Apparently satisfied, the leathery old matriarch taps the side of her head, points at my face and undulates away. She likes the Cayman. She likes the fixed rear spoiler. She likes the massaged bodywork, the mascara'd black of the headlight-surrounds. She likes the seventies graphics down the side, and she loves the lightweight black wheels. She even likes the interior, trimmed as it is in blood-

SA CALOBRA

▲ ·········· Puig Major

PANTA DE
GORGE BLAU

leather and white plastic like some sort of futuristic abattoir. Probably.

What she doesn't know is that if it were down to pure rationale, there would appear to be very little point in the R. Compared to a standard Cayman S, it's a bit lower, a tiny bit faster, a smidge more powerful by 10bhp – though torque remains the same – has more downforce (15 per cent at the front, and 40 per cent at the rear) and a tad less weight. I'll admit that 55kg of weight reduction is significant in a car of this size, bringing down the total to 1,295kg, but probably not a deal-breaker.

To get there, the R deletes the aircon and radio to save 15kg, gains aluminium doors, lightweight wheels and CFRP bucket seats to save 15kg, 5kg and 12kg respectively, adopts a slightly smaller fuel tank and loses a few other niceties like interior doorhandles – replaced by GT3 RS-style fabric loops – and cup-holders to save the remainder. Most of which, incidentally, you can then option *back in*. If you also option a PDK gearbox – which weighs 25kg more than a standard six-speed manual – the R ends up weighing pretty much the same as a lightly optioned S. With only around 10bhp more.

So what's the point? Bragging rights? Possibly. Personally, I'd probably buy the R package for the seats and interior trim alone, so wickedly perfect are they, but so far, dynamically, it just feels like a Cayman with a peculiarly sympathetic suspension set-up. It's impossible to tell anything more significant, simply because of the ridiculous aggregation of factors denying me a decent drive. It's 2am, and Jamie the photographer and I finally admit defeat and return to the hotel, ever so slightly broken. No road on Mallorca. No fun.

During the night, I have a dream. And no, not that kind. I have a dream that Dan from the office emails me the location of a mythical road on Mallorca. An amazing driving road. A road not two hours from where we are. Confused as to whether dream emails actually count and fretting at the edges of sleep, I finally give in to the siren call, rouse Jamie and we head back out in the Cayman. It is 5.30am. Jamie does not look overly pleased.

Two hours of driving later, as we crest the top of a coastal mountain range and enter what can only be called low-lying cloud masquerading as dense pea-souper fog, Jamie has what we describe in the North of

FAR LEFT (OPPOSITE PAGE): *Just out of shot, an old lady wags her stick in approval of the Cayman. Must be the Seventies graphics*

LEFT: *At least one hundred bright red cows were sacrificed to make this interior. May they rest in peace*

BELOW: *Loud exhausts are perfect for waking up entire Spanish neighbourhoods. Who needs cockerels when you have a lightweight Porsche, eh?*

England as 'a slightly mardy face on'. No road. And now, as the sun starts to rise, no forward vision. Brilliant. Just brilliant. Hard to be phlegmatic when the cards are stacked and the capricious gods are pissed and feeling vindictive. But just as we're about to turn back, we roll around a wall of russet rock, the mist lifts, and...

...my eyes pop out of my head. It's like fumbling through the back of a musty wardrobe and plopping out in the lean, little Porsche's private Narnia. I coast to a stop at the top of the mountain road, lean forward over the steering wheel with hands gripping 11 and 1, and say things my mother would not be proud to hear. Ahead and below, across and down and away is the most stupefying road I have ever seen. The island valley opens itself like a book, and between the pages is a slick of bitumen designed by a madman. Or an artist. Ropes of tarmac hang loosely around the shoulders of the mountain like an indifferent noose, trailing down the side of the hill in lazy loops. There are straights and curves and switchbacks and even, at one ridiculous point, a loop where the road curves back, around and under itself like a bow.

Not only is this vision wrought in civil engineering perfectly surfaced, free of potholes and shimmying traction changes, it is utterly, bleakly empty. Not a damn soul. Turns out this road, this awesome Sa Colobra road, is a dead end, servicing a small seaside town at its watery terminus. Hit it at the right time of day – ridiculously early in the morning, say – and you have the place to yourself. At last.

I look right and down the first section, prod Sport, Exhaust and PASM off on the dash, slot first and dump the clutch. I then stop again, remove the handbrake, and repeat, leaving in the kind of dramatic fishtail you only ever see in Seventies B-movies. It feels good. Scratch that, it feels *incredible*. What follows is a dirty blur of exhilaration. For the first time, the Cayman R is allowed its head, rearing towards the right-hand side of the rev-counter, the breathy freedom of modified exhaust-headers finally announcing their presence.

The gearbox snaps a little clunkily once, twice, three times, before the road ducks right, down and back, so the standard steel brakes are forced into heavy work early on, dipping the nose of the Cayman, forcing it to snort hard at the tarmac. The exhaust woofles and pops, amplified by the rocks to the left, just as the gradient tries to suck the rear of the car away from the apex. But nothing happens except an insane increase in lateral *g*. The Cayman's steering places it

perfectly, the front end staying true, even when you would forgive it for wandering. And all the time, the road reveals a little more of itself in a teasingly burlesque fashion, glimpses of hairpins, flirty little hints of racetrackish madness. I miss two downchanges simply by becoming lost in the view.

Very much like the Nordschleife, there's no rhythm to this road, no easy cadence. Corners tighten from regular radii down to last-gasp 90-degree bends that have your buttocks puckering so tightly they begin to gum at the Alcantara of the seats. Some parts flow and allow you speed, others have you chunking through second and third like your life depends on it, the Cayman's tail slewing wide in glorious unfettered arcs. The standard-fit limited-slip differential helps, nudging the nose forwards into understeer and then allowing you to punt the rear away, never quite getting past a half-turn of countersteer. It is, without being overly emotional about it, sublime. Truthfully? I'm not that good a driver, but there's something about this Cayman R that sells you on the idea of invincibility.

You sit in the middle, with the engine close behind, and you become the pivot. This is no pendulous 911 – no matter how well disguised that car's dynamic shortcomings have become – and the Cayman R is genuinely small, reliably connected and utterly faithful. It's a Cayman with added salt and pepper – the basic meal is satisfyingly the same, but the flavour has been subtly and significantly improved. There are very, very few cars you would dare drive this hard on this kind of road, a road where a slip, or a snap of oversteer, would likely prove expensively bloody. The Cayman R is one of them. There are no surprises. Just joy.

After what seems like an age, but is in reality little more than an hour, it starts to rain. We have traversed this little 10-mile stretch of brilliance to the sea and halfway back, but with a light smattering of water on salty tarmac, the surface becomes slick and treacherous. After one flail to the lockstops and back while staring at a rock wall through the passenger window, I opt for discretion over valour, dry-swallow my heart and pick my way back over the mountain. Back to real life. And just before I swing around that last corner and disappear into the cloudy mist, I look down the valley and grin like a horse-faced loon. One of the world's best secret roads, just made for a car like the Porsche Cayman R, on a tiny island like Mallorca. It's easy. You just have to know where to look.

HIGH AND MIGHTY

JAMES MAY DRIVES A CONVERTIBLE MCLAREN UP THE HIGHEST ROAD IN EUROPE. TIME TO DROP THE TOP

have never quite understood the widespread accusations of dullness levelled at McLaren's MP4-12C supercar. I think it springs from timid cultural conventions.

The thinking seems to go that the phenomenon of The Supercar – by which we really mean the Italian supercar – comes at a price; a price that those of us admitted to the inner sanctum accept as a rite of entry. We even boast about it. Supercars come with awkward boots, shocking blind spots, low-speed cussedness, stupid options lists, quirky transmissions, terrifying repair bills following minor mishaps, baffling control logic, and all the rest of it. The McLaren doesn't really offer any of this, and therefore must be 'a bit boring'.

But hang on. 'My supercar is great to drive, works properly and is easy to own' is not the ranting of a pub dullard. There's a deep and largely unfamiliar pleasure to be taken in a truly high-performance car that works exactly as advertised. And in any case, it doesn't *quite* work perfectly, but we'll come on to that.

Battling my way up Europe's highest paved road in the Sierra Nevada, I am reminded of everything I found deeply satisfying about the McLaren the first time I drove it, on *TopGear* telly. The fidelity of that gearchange, the even weighting of all the controls, the ease of driving really quite fast, the intelligent way the reconfiguration of the engine output and chassis set-up is separated. It's all good. It's great fun mocking Ron Dennis's po-faced Wokingshire anal retentiveness about detail, but do you know what? He might be on to something.

And now, as we would normally say of Dacia, there's

WHERE IS IT?
Up in the Sierra Nevada Mountains

WHICH BIT?
From Grenada to Hoya de la Mora

GIVE ME CO-ORDINATES!
37.128553, -3.427016

WHEN SHOULD I GO?
After the snow and before the cyclists. March should do it

HOW LONG WILL IT TAKE?
An hour or so each way

HOW DO I GET THERE?
Get a cheap flight to Grenada

WHAT'S THE WEATHER LIKE?
Spanish

WHAT'S THE ROAD LIKE?
Bendy

WHAT IF I GET LOST?
At 3,384 metres high, you can probably see your house from the top

TG TOP TIP:
The road is usually closed to general traffic beyond the ski station…

ONE MORE THING:
…but you can request special permission to drive to the summit, or swap for a bicycle

GOOD NEWS! The McLaren MP4-12C has been improved. First up, it's now available in this Spider form, with the accepted folding hard-top. As the car was conceived from the outset this way, there's no compromise in rigidity or even bootspace, and the weight penalty of the various motors and rods that effect the transformation is just 40kg. The roof, which can be raised on the move at speeds of up to *precisely* 24.8548mph, is one of the fastest in the business, lowering completely in just 17 seconds. Ambient temperature apparently has a small impact on the exact time, and I don't really know why, but I'm bloody impressed that they are in a position to tell me that. They're thorough, this lot.

The name has changed, too. Recognising that MP4-12C sounded a bit like one of the upgradable components of a desktop PC, McLaren simply calls the car the 12C. So this is the McLaren 12C Spider.

That daft and faintly ritualistic way of opening the doors has gone too. There is now a discreet button to press, and it works every time, saving you from the embarrassment of mincing about like a bad kerbside mime artist performing a routine about a giant invisible iPhone. This change, apparently, was 'in response to customer requests'; the request probably being, 'Please get rid of that stupid door-opening system or I'm buying a Lamborghini.'

There's more. Power is up several notches from

Armilla

GRANADA

Huétor Vega

Cenes de la Vega

Pinos Genil

KIOSKO BAR HOYA DE LA MORA

592bhp to 616bhp, the sound of the exhaust can be altered independently of the setting selected on the power knob, and the gearchange software has been mildly tweaked for even more synaptic reactions. The 12C Spider does, however, lose 1mph in outright speed to the coupe, which may have kept Ron awake for several months.

Finally, and after a year or more of foot-shuffling and 'Don't know, Sir', the touchscreen central pod now incorporates satnav. This is one of the things onto which I wanted to come, as promised earlier.

McLaren's satnav has been the maths homework of the supercar world, in several ways. Determined to develop its own software instead of buying perfectly good off-the-shelf stuff, it has undoubtedly involved quite a lot of maths. And, like all maths homework that I ever did, it's not finished.

It's not just that it sometimes crashed and locked me resolutely into a small village even though I'd long since roared off into the mountains. The angle of the screen is such that with the roof down and the sun anywhere overhead, you simply can't see it. This means you have to cup a free hand around it to make out the picture, leaving you with no free hand to touch the screen. And while the rest of the electronic interface is simpler and more logical than a Ferrari 458's, the satnav is convoluted.

I don't really want to go on about this. Yes I do. Developing your own satnav software in a world already oversupplied with excellent satnav software is a bit like trying to cook your own Indian food. It takes ages, and it's still crap compared with the stuff from the nearest restaurant.

Still, it's good to know that even Ron Dennis is fallible, and that even his supercar can have exclusively supercar-like foibles. Although there's always a chance that he did this deliberately to confound his critics.

Another issue is that the buffeting around the headrest is a bit extreme at high speeds. Yet another is that, owing to the way the door opens and the rake of the windscreen, any 12C is a bit awkward to get in and out of. Long agoI recognised that I was too old to drive a convertible with any dignity.

LEFT: *High up in the Spanish Sierra Nevada, James points an accusatory finger at the McLaren's satnav controls*

LEFT (OPPOSITE PAGE): *You want long, sweeping corners that go on forever? You've come to the right place! Now all you need is a car*

BELOW: *This is the highest paved road in the whole of Europe, where bulls roam free, unaware of fast-approaching television presenters*

Now I'm beginning to look too old to *leave* one with any dignity, or indeed any impression of innate balance. The force that through the green fuse drives the flower is driving my green age, and it's depressing to discover that driving a supercar reveals it so utterly.

Anyway. We're up in the mountains, and no one would be able to see my penis if I were driving this car naked with the top down, and, by my own rules, that means I'm allowed to drop the roof. Once it's down, the 'tonneau' part behind the seats can be raised again to reveal a second small boot. The vertical glass between the seats can be raised and lowered independently. Lower it but keep the side windows up if driving fast. This seems to give the smoothest airflow in the cabin.

The heater is cracking and so are the heated seats. Off we go, then. Select manual control, set the chassis and power knobs to Sport and Track respectively, the McLaren 12C Spider is instantly alive and eager.

The great thing about the 12C is that it's easy to drive. It's probably the most benign supercar I've ever tried. Again, some would want to be admired for their courage in mastering a Ferrari GTO or the demanding Aventador, but I say cobblers to that. I can challenge myself by learning to play the violin. This is a good-time car and I want a good time. I get it.

At first, and having recently stepped from a Ferrari 458, I thought that the McLaren's steering had become even quicker and more nervous. But I'm assured that nothing in the undercarriage has been changed, so it must just be the air.

What definitely has changed is the engine, the nature of which was always central to the dark mutterings that said the McLaren was a bit boring; the quantity surveyor standing in the kitchen of the supercar party. Various tweaks to engine mapping – God knows what, and for once I'm with Clarkson and *literally* not interested – have made the twin-turbo V8 really quite barking mad. The exemplary low-range grunt is now complemented by the right sort of noise – a bit grubby, like a dirty laugh from a buxom wench in a period-drama tavern. Or something like that.

This engine – and this is as it should be – defines the essential character of the McLaren and perfectly distinguishes it from the 458. They are very different, and no one should dismiss the Woking operation as Britain's

attempt to have its own Maranello. Apart from anything else, have you ever been to Woking?

The Ferrari's engine is fizzy, raspy and brittle. It encourages a foray into its upper reaches. The McLaren motor is gruff and woofly, and likes a short shift so it can growl at you. The Ferrari is like a slightly yappy terrier, the McLaren like a faintly bad-tempered bloodhound. The Ferrari is histrionic, while there's a bit of floppy-eared harrumphing about the McLaren. It's slightly friendlier, despite seeming like a more clinical and academic proposition in the first place.

To put it another way, the Ferrari experience is quite cool and a bit artistic. It's like handling an exquisitely sculpted statue. The McLaren is more like fondling a real human being; warmer and more comforting. This is the opposite of what popular preconception would suggest.

It's now no secret – although the man from McLaren didn't know, so I didn't mention it – that I own a 458. Even at the last minute, I wondered if the McLaren might be the more knowing choice. I still wonder sometimes, and when a man tweeted me the other day to tell me he'd ordered the car formerly known as the MP4-12C, I couldn't readily respond with a Ferrari-centric put-down. There isn't one. The McLaren is a terrific car.

I enjoyed one of those once-in-a-motoring-lifetime experiences driving up the mountains. The road was cut deftly into the rock face as if with one wandering stroke from the divine carpenter's rebating tool. The cloud that we'd been promised was rolling up the steep slope to my right, driven by the Sierra Nevada's notorious winds. Then the cloud crossed the road, but didn't drop into it. I found myself driving along the internal, horizontal side of a tunnel formed like the right-angled triangle of a geometry exercise, framed on the other two sides by the vertical rock face and the slanting canopy of solid white not 10 feet above my head. It was the driving equivalent of what I think is known as 'piping' in surfing circles. I've never been more pleased to find myself in a car without a roof.

It was truly magical, lasting for maybe two minutes. Long enough for me to wonder if the experience could have been improved by a different car. It couldn't, to be honest. The McLaren 12C, in all its forms, is tremendous.

Maybe the only thing keeping me in a Ferrari is that I can get out of it more easily.

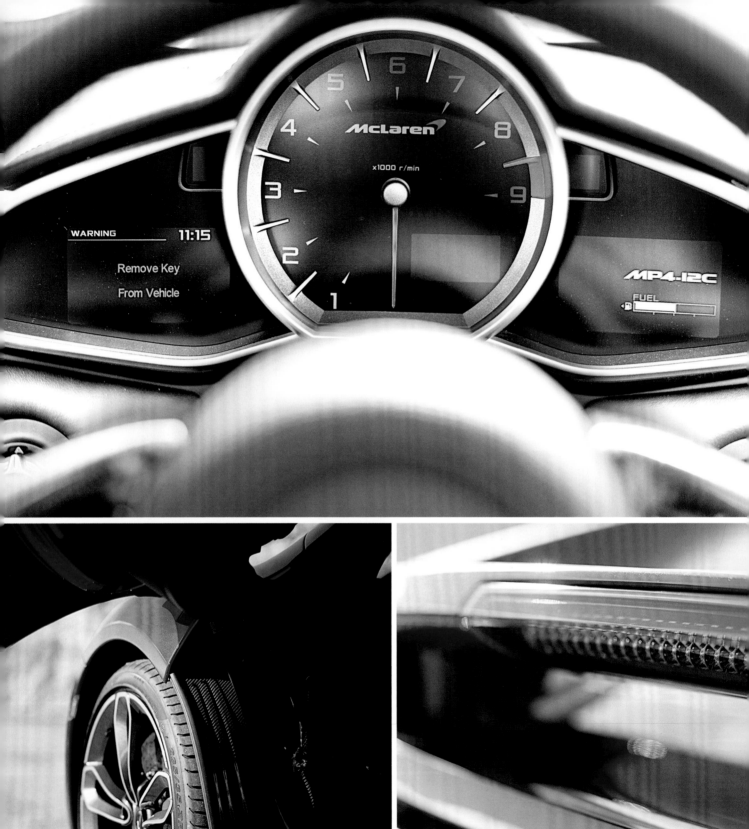

NORSE POWER

THE JAGUAR XKR-S IS A SPECIAL CAR IN NEED OF A SPECIAL ROAD. THANKFULLY, THE NORWEGIANS MADE SURE IT GOT ONE

I know one word in Norwegian, and that word is *stengt*. It means 'closed'. The reason I know this is because *stengt*, the monosyllabic, guttural little bugger, has just massacred a Big *TopGear* Road Trip in a single blow.

Ten minutes ago, all was sweetness and light as we merrily closed in on the Lysebotnveien, a physics-defying mountain road that has become something of a *TG* obsession. Somewhere outside Tonstad, as the snow by the roadside was piling deeper, photographer Wycherley politely asked whether I'd checked if the Lysebotn road was actually open, and I said don't be daft, of course I checked, and anyhow, why on earth would a hairy mountain pass be closed in spring and... and then there was a long pause followed by some frantic fiddling with phones and a lot of swearing. A couple of minutes

later, here it is in undeniable capitals. Lysebotnveien: *STENGT*. Thanks to Norway's odd obsession with getting snowed on, the planned end point of our trip has been closed since October and isn't due to open for another fortnight. *Stengt!*

So you join us at a small, overpriced petrol station, panic-eating our way through three kilos of Firkløver, Japp and Kvikk Lunsj – Norway's finest triumvirate of chocolate bars – with a 542bhp super-coupe grunting impatiently on the forecourt and nowhere to go.

This is what happens when you try to meet your heroes. Our Lysebotn obsession started with a YouTube clip of BASE jumpers throwing themselves wantonly from a kilometre-high, perfectly vertical Norwegian cliff. Just visible in the background was a sliver of road cut

WHERE IS IT?
In the south western fjords

WHICH BIT?
From Lysebotn to Sirdal

GIVE ME CO-ORDINATES!
59.050336, 6.659055

WHEN SHOULD I GO?
Definitely not between October and April-ish, when it's closed. We learned this the hard way

HOW LONG WILL IT TAKE?
An hour, if you don't crash

HOW DO I GET THERE?
No direct ferries from the UK these days, so it's a short flight or a long drive via mainland Europe

WHAT'S THE WEATHER LIKE?
Scandi

WHAT'S THE ROAD LIKE?
Slippery

WHAT IF I GET LOST?
Call 001 for fire, 002 for police and 003 for an ambulance

TG TOP TIP:
In Norway, even creeping over the speed limit can land you a hefty fine. Slower is safer, and cheaper…

ONE MORE THING:
Should you notice a large thump on your roof, it's probably an errant BASE jumper. It's a popular sport around here

deep into the rock face, snaking back and forth to the cliff top. After literally some seconds of intensive research, we located the road on Google Maps, and it was even more astonishing than we'd hoped: 30 hairpins laced up the sheer side of a fjord, a clear contender for Greatest Road in the World. In one of those moments of lateral thinking for *TopGear* is renowned, we came up with a plan: wouldn't it be a fine idea to drive a fast car, fast, on the Lysebotn road?

But, like the posh bottle of red wine that sits gathering dust on the shelf because you can never find exactly the right occasion to drink it, I decided just any old fast car wouldn't do for this road. It had to be the right car, the perfect car: a car capable of soaking up the cross-country schlep to the westernmost edge of Norway, but equally capable of teaching those hairpins some manners at the other end. Many, many suggestions were made; all were rejected – no car was good enough for my super-road.

And then Jaguar launched the XKR-S – a turn-all-the-knobs-up-to-11 iteration of the already-lovely XKR – and the perfect road had its perfect car. It's important not to dive into these things with overblown expectations. And so, through means of pleading and deception, I did obtain Jag's very first XKR-S and set out in the direction of Norway, which is a very long way away from Fortress *TopGear*.

The XKR-S likes long ways. What a car this is. Despite packing 542bhp and a top speed of 186mph, it isn't, as the marketing types claim, the fastest and most powerful

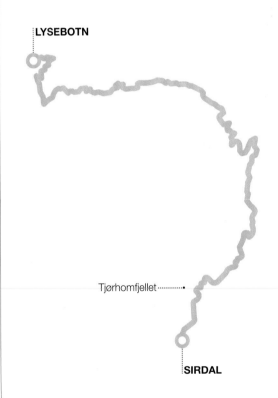

LYSEBOTN

Tjørhomfjellet

SIRDAL

Jaguar ever: 1991's XJ220 boasted the same power output and could manage 217mph flat out. Nor is it, despite the name, a pared-down, roll-caged rival to Porsche's 911 GT3 RS: there's more leather in the XKR-S's cabin than at a Hells Angel's funeral, along with a pair of occasional rear seats and a decent-sized boot under the rear hatch.

Nonetheless, the XKR-S is a razor-edged thing. On the outside, the most obvious mods are the fixed carbon-fibre rear wing and the vertical vents on either side of the XKR-S's gaping mouth. These don't do much for the coupe's svelte lines, but combine to reduce high-speed lift by 26 per cent. Bumping the 5.0-litre supercharged V8 from 510bhp – its output in the standard XKR – was a straightforward task, requiring nothing more than an engine remap and exhaust tweak, but the chassis was subjected to heftier revisions. The double-wishbone front suspension has been toughened up, increasing camber and castor stiffness, the springs are 26 per cent sharper all round, and lightweight 20in alloys reduce unsprung weight by five kilograms over the XKR. It all adds up to a 4.2-second 0–62mph time and, says Jaguar, a sub-eight-minute Nordschleife lap.

Never the types to sniff at extra power and focus and wings, we had a momentary worry that the XKR-S might be treading a slightly tricky path. The XKR has always steered clear of the track-focused, performance-car fist fight, instead carving out a niche as a super-fast grand tourer. With this talk of 'Ring laps, might the sleek Jag have forgotten its USP?

Not to worry. Even in this gym-honed guise, the XKR-S retains Jaguar's trademark delicacy of ride. On Norway's wide, sweeping roads, flashing past glittering pine forests and wide lakes with sunlight splintering off the water's surface, the XKR-S was firm but never harsh, planted but pliable. Yes, it's noticeably stiffer than the XKR, but never crunching or brittle. No company does damping better than Jaguar... and no company makes a better supercharged engine.

What a unit this big V8 is, capable of buttery relaxation or wild-eyed redline-chasing. In tandem with the six-speed ZF transmission, it's a welcome riposte to anyone who thinks the conventional auto 'box is dead: slick-shifting and anonymous when left to do its own thing, fast and direct when you override with the steering-wheel paddles.

So we know the XKR-S devours miles like a Scandinavian trucker devours pickled fish, but – because some idiot forgot to check whether a road was open – we have no idea what it's like on wiggly stuff. I take a rueful nibble of Japp and wonder how long it'd take to fashion a snow plough for the front of an XKR-S. A clang from

LEFT: *OK, we checked. These surroundings are definitely not safe. Times like these call for another mouthful of Firkløver!*

FAR LEFT (OPPOSITE PAGE): *Sharp cliffs, slippery road, one rare and expensive coupe from just outside Birmingham. What could possibly go wrong?*

BELOW: *In many ways, Norway is very much like Scotland. Only warmer, better and much less deep-fried*

my phone. An email from a nice lady somewhere in the Norwegian tourism office who has talked to a nice man in the Norwegian roads department. They work quickly, these Vikings. The nice man in the Norwegian roads department says sorry for the inconvenience, and if we wouldn't mind terribly hanging around until tomorrow morning, he'll clear all the snow away for us and we can have the road to ourselves. The first car on the Lysebotn road in eight months. Couldn't have planned it better. In celebration, we polish off a Firkløver between us.

It is tomorrow morning, and the XKR-S is about to play vicar in the Lysebotn road's yearly christening. The barrier is up, the tarmac is clear, and there is not a human for miles around. As we turn off the main road onto the single-lane Lysebotnveien, a fat, brown snake slimes lazily from the verge. I'm no expert on omens, but that can't be a good one.

Twisting between granite moraines and icy lakes, we climb and climb, the damp-green vegetation fading to snow. The sky is heavy, the scenery magnificent and other-worldly, brutal and beautiful. You can see how Norse mythology became so rich and weird: it's easier to imagine this landscape being shaped by temperamental deities than by the actions of mere wind and water. The XKR-S picks its way light-footedly along the skinny path.

Higher still. More snow. Blizzards sweep at pace across the ridge, pummelling the car and drifting snow onto the road. Drops of tens, hundreds of feet loom inches from the roadside, plunging away into half-frozen pools and craggy precipices. Rear-wheel drive and 542bhp doesn't feel like the most sensible choice now. Credit to the Jag: it soldiers on without fuss. It's astonishingly effective at getting its power down, this car, rarely troubling the traction-control system unless you give the accelerator a proper volley. We squeeze between snowbanks 12ft high, the gap barely wider than the XKR-S, and I wonder if, rather than revealing itself to be the greatest road in the world, the Lysebotnveien might turn out to be an utterly stupid idea instead.

And then we dive down below the snowline and the clouds lift and suddenly we are at the edge of a cliff and hanging over a vista that sends the blood rushing to the fingertips and leaves a half-formed expletive hanging in the throat. We are at the brink of the Lysefjord, a vicious, kilometre-deep cut through the landscape, fringed by

looming towers of rock and the frothing North Sea. The road plunges over the cliff-edge and the XKR-S launches into the abyss.

Does it get any better than this? Skimming from hairpin to hairpin on this astonishing road, V8 crackling off the cliffs, against a backdrop that can only be described as Sigur-Rós-soundtrack-made-real. Each hairpin is subtly different, some tightening, some widening, some off-camber, but every one is as impeccably surfaced as a just-laid race circuit. The XKR-S is loving it. For a big front-engined car, it's surprisingly wieldy, tucking neatly into the corners and, even on this cold, damp tarmac, clinging on with the tenacity of an emotionally dependent limpet. Get on the power early, and the rear tyres give a quick twitch before hooking up all that power, the Jag simply hurling itself down the straight and into the next corner.

Perfect? It's not far off. The only dynamic question mark is over the steering. Slowed slightly for added stability at the extreme speeds the XKR-S is capable of, the wheel is a touch short of feel. It's still accurate, but there's just a lack of feedback which, when you're trying to guess how much grip you've got left at the front, is a mite disconcerting. A minor issue, but there's a more major one. A £97,000 issue, to be precise, a price that (at the time of writing) puts the XKR-S a whopping £20,000 above the XKR and into direct competition with some very grown-up metal: the Audi R8 V10, a kitted-out 911 GT3, and the Aston Martin Vantage S. Serious company but, with its supernatural breadth of abilities and monstrous power reserves, the XKR-S justifies its lofty price tag.

And here comes its party trick. Down into second gear, and into the tunnel. Did I not mention the tunnel? Well, you know how all greatest roads must have, by law, both hairpins and tunnels? The Lysebotn road combines the two, boasting a roughly hewn borehole that burrows half a mile straight under the mountain before turning 180 degrees and bolting for daylight. Deep under the mountain now, braking hard for the hairpin. Very weird experience. Back on the power. No margin for error here: the metal markers, warning of the jagged tunnel walls, flit within inches of the XKR's wing mirrors. The tarmac is uneven and damp, and the speed is rising. Past 4,500rpm, and something dark and magical happens deep within the Jag's exhaust. The bassy bellow rises to an unholy supercharged scream, the entire tunnel reverberating as we are spat out back into the light. What a noise. What a car. And – when it's open – what a road.

ØYGARDSTØL

Eagle's Nest

Kjerag Panoramic
Restaurant and Cafe

THE PATH TO ENLIGHTENMENT

ACROSS ICELAND IN SEARCH OF ZEN, USING ONLY A STRANGELY COLOURED CACTUS AND AN OPEN MIND. CAN A CAR REALLY HELP YOU FIND INNER PEACE?

Here I am, semi-naked in a cave, being observed by a wide-eyed and tungsten-headed division of elderly German tourists. They look surprised to find me floating nearly nude in an underground geothermal hot spring somewhere in the back country of eastern Iceland, but, then again, this isn't your average Wednesday morning. This Wednesday, I am attempting to find instant inner peace. Purest calm before tomorrow. Elysium before teatime. To do so, I have travelled to the spiritual expanse of Iceland – a country I've always found to be emotionally soothing – and have had two days to reboot my misfiring chakras and enlighten my cynical soul. It's not working. I've got to be at another enlightenment appointment in an hour, and thanks to recent geological disturbances, this pool is so warm that

it feels like I'm being boiled alive. The so-called healing water is 45+ degrees Celsius. Much more healing, and I'll have second-degree burns, which means that I'm unlikely to find much Zen outside of a specialist treatment unit. I retreat, somewhat pinkly, to my secret weapon in the search for serenity – a lime-green Citroen C-Cactus.

I know what you're thinking. How can a car named after a stabby plant possibly provide a path to tranquillity? Well, this little Citroen has placidity at its core. It's been designed to be friendly and simple and calm. To abdicate responsibility for the arms race of complexity that plagues carmakers, to revert to the straightforward. Strip away the unnecessary, concentrate on making the important stuff better and, in the process, cook up an antidote to overly elaborate, stressful design. In other words, make it cheap and simple

WHERE IS IT?
The North Atlantic

WHICH BIT?
From Reykjavik to Krafla Power Station

GIVE ME CO-ORDINATES!
65.463418, -18.813807

WHEN SHOULD I GO?
Give yourself a chance and go in summertime,
around the solstice, for some midnight sun

HOW LONG WILL IT TAKE?
Two or three days, there and back

HOW DO I GET THERE?
You could swim, but an aeroplane is more
advisable. Rent a 4x4 from Reykjavik airport

WHAT'S THE WEATHER LIKE?
Bleak

WHAT'S THE ROAD LIKE?
Black

WHAT IF I GET LOST?
Route 1 is a giant ring road that laps the island. So
you'll always end up back where you started

TG TOP TIP:
You could carry on to the fjords in the east. Stay
in Reydarfjördur, where they filmed the telly show
Fortitude

ONE MORE THING:
This is the land of overpriced alcohol, but it's possible
to find a cheap pint at Dillon Bar in Reykjavik

but satisfying. A tricky mission statement when many
measure a car's worth based on Byzantine functions they
never use – after all, 'simple' is a word not too far from
'utilitarian'. And 'utilitarian' often translates badly.

Still, on the outside, the Cactus doesn't look dull.
Anything but. It looks like a conceptual mini-SUV, with
a semi-raised ride height, squinty eyes and lots of visual
jewellery. There are shades of the Picasso in there and
bold Citroen chevrons. The raised rectilinear blisters on
the side are called Airbumps and really are little squishy
pockets designed to absorb the kind of supermarket
door scuffs that annoy beyond reason. The roof rails add
a bit of square-jawed ruggedness, and the 'floating roof'
looks vogueish and contemporary but is accomplished
by the slightly more prosaic method of falsely wrapping
the windowline around the car with swathes of black
plastic. But it looks fresh and interesting and more than
a little bit exciting – certainly more entertaining than a
conventional hatch.

Which is exactly what it is below the skin. Don't let
the stance and style fool you: underneath, the C-Cactus
is a version of the C3/Peugeot 208 platform, a mass-
produced, well-proven base. There are MacPherson
struts for the front suspension and a simple torsion bar
in the rear, and the biggest engine available produces
a humble 109bhp. Which is the one we have here.
You can specify a more conventional turbodiesel
four-cylinder, but the petrol engines in the C-Cactus
are all versions of a turbocharged 1.2-litre three-

KRAFLA POWER STATION

Akureyri

Skagaströnd

Sauðárkrókur

Akrahreppur

Hvammstangi

Borgarnes

Akranes

REYKJAVIK

cylinder with variously managed outputs, and the quirky-but-good three-pot seems appropriate. The offbeat thrum of the little motor certainly suits the car, and as we haul away from the cave bath and lightly appalled European pensioners up one of eastern Iceland's long, sweeping uphill roads, the little turbo whooshes along most satisfactorily. It's not fast by any means, and there are only five speeds available from the floppy manual gearbox, but somehow it doesn't seem to matter. Immediately, it's a happy little thing.

We track out and along the top part of some of the Icelandic back country, overtaking lumbering, hugely tyred local super trucks and dawdling hired Toyota hatchbacks, making both seem by turn immensely archaic and intensely boring. The countryside beats up and down in a smooth black lava oscillation, a massive, ancient geological heartbeat – the main road cutting through it like a single tarmac main artery feeding innumerable veins of gravelly, unmade tracks. We're on our way to a place where I can look into the future. A future in which a low-impact, efficient little car like the Cactus will fit very nicely.

On the way, I have time to think. Iceland's a bit like that. It's

a beautiful but brutal island, measured in muted tones, scarred by the violence of its conception. And it makes you prone to a kind of slightly dark contemplation. There is no daylight in the winter months, and now, in summer, night time is just a slight greying of the horizon. Not sure which is worse. I've only been here a couple of days, and it's already starting to mess with my head. It must be, because despite my obsession with horsepower, I'm starting to really fall for the Cactus, and it has approximately 400 less bhp than I usually require to fuel my ego. It's pretty obvious from the driving experience that, underneath the 'simplification over complication' PR spin, this is just a C3 with a glittery frock, but the Cactus really will be cheap in some versions – starting at just under £13k – and it's really wonderfully characterful for that. A little pod of soft, friendly vibes. Hard not to feel comforted by it, in this place.

One of the reasons is that the Cactus feels… light. Both physically and emotionally. The styling doesn't take itself too seriously, and everyone we meet seems happily interested in it. It's unthreatening but not comical, interesting but not pastiche. There's a huge glass roof that saves 6kg over conventional steel sheet and makes the car feel open and airy, and the rear bench doesn't split or

FAR LEFT (OPPOSITE PAGE): *The world's most remote waterslides, or the Krafla Power Station? There's only one way to find out: fetch your swimming trunks!*

LEFT: *Inside, the cabin is smart and funky. The only worry is if that screen fails in five years' time.*

BELOW: *If we told you this picture was taken on a future Moon base, would you believe us? Thought not.*

slide, saving precious weight. Most pointlessly electrified functions make do with manual adjustment, with only the front windows being electric and the rears hingeing out a couple of inches. Sounds annoying, but electric motors are heavy, and the lack of wind-down rear windows saves 11kg and allows the rear doors to be sculpted for more elbow-room, so the car always feels roomy, even if it's 20cm shorter and 6cm narrower than a C4. The result is that the Cactus really is, by modern standards, a featherweight. In fact, this little acid green Citroen (the official colour is 'Hello Yellow', but it looks green to me) only weighs about a tonne. Anything with this interior volume generally weighs about a fifth more, which means that the modest engine range doesn't need to work hard to motivate the car. It also means that the Cactus can have smaller brakes, less need for cooling and a lighter drivetrain – it's a virtuous circle that means it feels peppy without ever troubling the limits of a somewhat modest handling capability. Indeed, Iceland's big sweeping curves do little to dispel the notion that the Cactus has any pretension to being fun to drive, and the endless uphills suck the momentum right out of the little car and require a downchange and revs to keep the little engine whirring in its powerband. There's not much for the keen driver here. But there's still something about the little Citroen that means it keeps your faith. It's an interesting little thing, plucky and fun, and I'm starting to come to the conclusion that there's something of the Fiat Panda about it. Small and cheap but not boring or thoughtless. And there would be definite possibilities for a proper Cactus AWD, or some sort of low-mu traction control and winter tyres, at least. I'm still thinking when we come across our next stop – the Krafla geothermal powerplant.

It looks like a Mars landing station. Silver and orange geodesic domes linked by swooping lines of pipes that race across the dusty, reddish-tinted earth like 22nd-century transit tubes. The main building looks like a modern museum, billowing clouds of sulphurous, artistic steam that smell disconcertingly of very rotten eggs. The best bit is that this is the industrial equivalent of the Cactus: using existing resources creatively. It looks like science fiction but has a far more unpretentious premise. In fact, it's bafflingly simple: Krafla is one of Iceland's original geothermal power stations, producing 60MW of power, and is basically a big heat exchanger

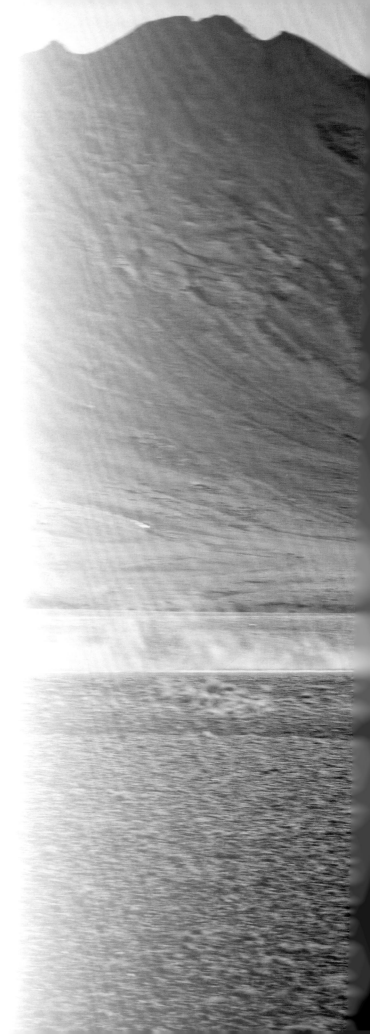

dropped on the top of the Krafla volcano. It uses 33 boreholes to drop water onto Iceland's volcanic undercarriage to produce steam, and, in turn, electricity. Places like this do a lot for my inner peace by assuaging my inherent motoring guilt. If we could make more of hot rocks, maybe I could offset my V8 habit a little. But even this isn't hitting the spot. I'm not nearing nirvana, despite being intrigued and comforted by super-green technology.

Back to the Cactus, and I'm starting to get a headache from the pressure to remain calm. Which is self-defeating. But the little Citroen helps. No, there are no heated seats or massively complex infotainment systems, but the interior is pared back, and the better for it, much like the view. There's a pleasing lack of buttons, most controls grouped into a single 7in touchscreen on the top of the dash, with a little LCD panel in front of the driver that displays basic info. The rest is given over to handy storage and the luxury – in a small car anyway – of space. There's a decent top-mounted glovebox on the dash, made possible by a passenger airbag that's disappeared up into the roof behind the sun visor, and big, wide, comfortable seats up front and a squashy

bench in the back – if you get the ETG auto 'box, you even get a sociable one-piece front seat. There's a slight worry that if the touchscreen decides to die in five years, then you'll only be able to operate the heated rear window, but generally it allows you to concentrate on pottering about without getting stressed because you can't find the right setting for the adaptive cruise control.

We head out to Lake Mývatn, and Iceland suddenly becomes a lot greener. There's not exactly an abundance of ancient forest, but the general ambience gently segues from black lava and sand the colour of dried blood to more healthy hues. Water. That'll do it. We stop, and I gaze out over the flat, glassy tranquillity of the lake, whose waters are punctuated by odd-looking pillars and arches of lava left from when the lake first appeared 2,300 years ago. I breathe deeply and try to find some sort of yogic centre, only to imagine that I look like I'm having a light asthma attack. There's one problem. My contemplation of the gentle majesty of age in nature is somewhat disturbed by having the local fauna stuffed up my nose, in my ears and dipping ceaselessly into my eyes. Flies. Endless swarms of tiny, personal-space-invading flies. I run around swatting at clouds of them like a loon, spitting them from my mouth and accidentally squashing them into my ears. It's enough to give you a phobia. And then I come across a helpful sign. Apparently 'mý' in Icelandic is 'midge'. And you'll have guessed already that 'vatn' means 'lake'. Nice view, but it's about as relaxing as being dipped in crawling insects. I retreat to a hotel, and night time grazes the horizon like a low-flying storm. Far from being more relaxed, I think I'm starting to lose it.

The next day, I track across wilder country, on unmade roads, and the Cactus throws up a few more surprises. The fact that the car is raised means that it rides well, and even running down a few light-hearted bits of off-roading, it deals with lumps and bumps without getting too fraught, which bodes well for the vagaries of sleeping policepersons in the UK. And while the little Citroen bobbles along, the views get bolder. We run along the side of a big hill, the path little more than a set of tyre tracks in red dust, and I suddenly realise that, as bizarre as it seems, the Cactus suits Iceland. What better car for a country that flips between lunar and Martian geography than one that looks like My First Spaceship? Much like the country, it makes use of known factors but somehow makes them look interesting, even if the underlying premise is simple. It has its own unique style, even though at first it feels a bit odd and unfamiliar. But, better than that, it brings things back to basics, without being beige. Up near the top of the hill, Iceland proves the same point. We round a corner, and spread below us is a view to make your brain stall.

In the near distance are volcanic vents that are pouring steam, hissing slightly. They're surrounded by glittering mineral deposits that phase from orange to yellow to red, and the water vapour in the air swirls little glistening rainbows around and about, highlighted against the dark smudge of the far horizon. The panorama is spread out in front like a painting, dipped in myriad shades. And it turns out that you don't need healing waters and technology to feel calm. You just need a big view and the time to enjoy it. Simple pleasures. It feels like freedom. Like peace. And the little, simple Citroen Cactus finally helped me get here.

ROSE-TINTED SPECTACLE

A GLORIOUS DAY WITH A BRIGHT RED FERRARI ON THE OPEN ROAD IN THE ITALIAN HILLS. *CHE BELLA...*

A cliché is often assumed to be a bad thing. An obvious stereotype, a bit lacking in imagination, something to be relied upon when you can't be bothered thinking of anything more creative. Except at this moment I'm fully submerged in cliché, and it feels utterly magnificent.

It's a red Ferrari – Rosso Corsa, to be pedantically exact – yowling with conspicuous pace through the hills above Maranello, Italy. The sun is buttery and warm across my face, even though it's late autumn, and there's a faint scent of woodsmoke and turned earth in the air. Local people smile, wave and encourage me to do antisocial things with the accelerator, just as you imagine they might do this close to Ferrari's birthplace. Cliché piled upon cliché in one glorious mess of typecasting. If Ferrari were to

make an advert using every hackneyed convention at its disposal, this would be it. Like I said, it feels damn fine.

It's made better because that woodsmoke is curling around the edges of a convertible Ferrari, a 458 Speciale Aperta. One of only 499 examples, as rare as the LaFerrari itself, or the 16M that preceded it, made available only to existing Ferrari collectors. It's pretty much as it says from the mouthful of a name: Aperta simply means 'open' in Italian, and this is the convertible hard-top variant of the hardcore 458 Speciale.

What that means is that this is a Spider with slightly more tangy venom than standard. The world's most powerful naturally aspirated V8 engine, converting air and fuel at a rate fast enough to produce 598bhp at 9,000rpm. There's 398lb ft of torque on offer, from an equally toppy

WHERE IS IT?
The heart of Italy

WHICH BIT?
Maranello to Mugello

GIVE ME CO-ORDINATES!
44.330152, 10.893903

WHEN SHOULD I GO?
Late summer or early autumn should be just about perfect

HOW LONG WILL IT TAKE?
This depends on how long you stop for lunch…

HOW DO I GET THERE?
From Bologna airport, take the E45 autostrada north-west to Modena, then head south

WHAT'S THE WEATHER LIKE?
Buttery

WHAT'S THE ROAD LIKE?
Knotty

WHAT IF I GET LOST?
Count your blessings and hope that nobody finds you. You're in heaven

TG TOP TIP:
Start with a tour of the Ferrari factory in Maranello, and look out for new cars testing in the hills

ONE MORE THING:
At the other end in Mugello, check out the old circuit and have a proper dinner at Gli Artisti Ristorante

---

6,000rpm – turbodiesel this is most certainly not – and the combination allows the 458 Speciale Aperta to wrinkle tarmac with abandon as it hits 62mph in just 3.0 seconds and 124mph in nine-and-a-half. Top speed is an OCD twitch-inducing 199mph. It weighs 50kg more than the Speciale Coupé, itself some 90kg less than its standard equivalent.

The weight-saving is an exercise in almost anal attention to detail, a long list of shaving and saving, paring and preserving. The engine needed new cams, higher valve lift, redesigned (shorter) inlet manifolds and different pistons to deal with the compression ratio of 14:1 (for a road car, that's impressive), and it got posher materials to make it actually weigh 8kg less than standard. Like the coupé, the Spider gets lighter, forged wheels (12kg saved), redesigned and lightened bodywork and glass (13kg gone) and a stripped interior (goodbye glovebox) to save another 20kg. Along with other mods, it adds up to the weight of a decent-sized passenger.

But the stats don't do it justice. To be honest, the increases in paper-based metrics over the standard 458 don't seem to warrant the bother. And yet, the Speciale Aperta feels very different to the standard Spider. Immediately. So you may have got an inkling from the extra vents and stripes on the outside, but it's not until you drive it that you realise how special the Speciale really is. Yes, it's docile enough through town – drop through a wormhole from 1970, and you'd fall over that a car with this much performance could be quite so easy to drive –

MARANELLO

Serramazzoni

Pavullo Nel Frignano

Marano

Porretta Terme

Castiglione dei Pepoli

Barberino di Mugello

MUGELLO

San Piero A Sieve

but once you nail the throttle with the roof down on a good road, your grin will circumnavigate your entire head.

First, the obvious stuff. With no roof, the sound has unfettered access to your eardrums, and it's *loud*. And far from the mad dash for gears of a turbocharged motor that snatches the horizon through the windscreen in a series of meaty grabs, this naturally aspirated engine, with its 9,000rpm lungs, seems to revel in each ratio that little bit longer. Stretching and pulling that noise through the scale, burnishing the octave to a shine with volume. Delicately pluck at the big, carbon scythe on the right-hand side of the steering wheel, and the car instantly bangs home another gear and repeats the process until the road – or your bravery – runs out. The seven-speed F1 double-clutch apparently matches revs even quicker than before, though in reality you only really sense that downshifts feel a bit more aggressive, and in moments, you'll be concentrating very hard indeed.

Find a corner, and you can snap downshifts with a crack from the exhaust, stamp hard on brakes and reverse momentum in a flash. Those brakes were developed with Brembo and apparently derived from lessons learned from the LaFerrari – smaller front pads made from HY 'hybrid' material latching onto HT2 discs with a higher percentage of silicon than before. According to Ferrari, the Speciale Aperta stops eight per cent faster than the 458 Spider. All I know is that you can brake hard enough to feel like you've been doing sit-ups all day. At one point, I seriously outbraked myself, absolutely committed to the stop, and the sunglasses fell off my face. Weirdly, we did get a small measure of fade, but the car we drove was extremely new, so possibly the brakes weren't fully bedded in. I think they probably were by the time we handed it back.

There's other stuff, too. The lack of a roof means that you hear the gearbox as it meshes gears – a brief, white-noise crash – and you can smell the carbon-ceramic of the brakes after a few hard stops. Hot metal and vaporised material. It's immersive in a way that the coupé isn't quite, although over a really bad road you might detect a slight shimmer of body movement you don't get with the hard-top. It's not enough to put you off: we certainly ran down some of the worst roads I've ever seen, and although the 458 should have been all over the place, it managed to keep composure. That's undoubtedly due to the Frequency-Shaped SCM-E dampers, this time equipped with twin solenoids and new software that modifies the magnetic field in the magnetorheological dampers every millisecond. Incredibly clever stuff that

ABOVE: *This is Ferrari country, just south of the factory, where future models can be seen testing on roads like these*

FAR LEFT: *Roof down – the only way to travel in the Aperta. Actually, you could keep it closed, but you'd be missing the point*

LEFT: *Yes, we know what you're thinking. It will be tricky to clean. But that's your butler's problem, eh?*

translates into an impressive ride – and if the bespoke Michelins are on the road, they're gripping and making you faster.

And gripping is something the Speciale does very well indeed, allowing you to play devastating tunes with that epic engine. Choose Race or CT Off from the manettino dial on the steering wheel, and Ferrari's Side Slip Angle Control works out how much sideways you can handle, and adjusts to suit. Basically, it looks at what you're doing, compares it with its reference data, and then torque-vectors between the two driven wheels using the e-diff. It makes heroes out of the average, and legends out of heroes. Mostly, though, the brilliant thing is that it just makes you feel like you did it yourself.

All the time, the car is feeding back, so there's no feeling of fakery or of insulation. To sound like a pretentious software engineer, or possibly a Ferrari press release, this doesn't feel like it has the electronics as a barrier, more an enabling technology. On one series of lovely, wide, second-gear Italian hairpins, on a dry road with third-gear squirts between them, the Speciale Aperta howled between like it was bungeed to the top of the hill. Accelerate, brake, turn, slide. Eat, sleep, race, repeat. It's rhythmic, and the change-up LEDs on the top circumference of the steering wheel become all the disco lights you ever want to see.

Again, there's a feeling of balance and of parity between all of the elements that make up this machine – it fits together on a very basic level, leaving you free to enjoy the experience. It's a 458, but more so. The steering is so well geared that the nose never dives for an apex, just naturally follows your eyes, feeds towards the corner. The car sets, and then you can layer in the power, feeling the lateral *g* build, until you sweep out of the other side with just a tweak of opposite lock. In fact, it's only when you switch it fully off that you realise how hard the bytes have been working – the back end comes around much more quickly, and will go all the way if you let it – though the mark of a well-balanced car in the first place is that it doesn't do so viciously. Amazing stuff in a mid-engined supercar.

The genius of it, more than anything, is that the Speciale Aperta feels like it really revels in what it's doing. To let that engine rev, to really hammer the brakes, turn in hard and brace your neck against the onslaught of forces, that's what this car is *for*. The world becomes a greeny-grey blur, more peripheral than anything else, your entire focus on scanning the road ahead. No wonder the Speciale looks a bit raptor-ish: when you get a little bit of red mist, the road just appears as prey.

There are a couple of things that grate. Surprising to say that, but it's true. First, there are a couple of plaques in the cabin, which feel really tacky. One just says LIMITED EDITION and looks like the kind of thing you get with a set of supposedly rare coins bought from the back of a Sunday supplement, and the other announces the V8's Engine of the Year awards. I also think that the more aerodynamically efficient rear end, with its twin exhausts either side of a blocky swathe of diffuser, is less elegant than the standard car's triple-pipe arrangement. I know it's for a measurable performance benefit, but it's just not quite as pleasing.

There's another sadness to the Speciale Aperta as well, and it's bittersweet. While parked on the side of the road staring at the car in the pictures, I could hear another sports car hammering down the same road. Not surprising really, seeing as these are Ferrari's test-driving routes. The car that eventually appeared was a white 458 covered in black gaffer tape and moving at an absolutely feral pace. As it went past, it whooshed, huffed and crackled – a good noise, but without doubt a turbocharged signature.

It's no particular secret that Ferrari is looking at smaller-capacity turbocharged engines for the next-generation 458, and although the car was obviously a rocket, and sounded fabulous, it didn't sound *the same*. I looked up at where the 458 T mule had disappeared off to, thought about giving chase, and then headed in the opposite direction instead. Back up into the hills, roof- off, desperate for one last blast.

That drive confirmed everything I suspected about this 458. That it's singular and superb and utterly magnificent, even though it's expensive and with a limited run. The removable roof simply adds another dimension to an already multi-faceted supercar, making it better, not worse. It doesn't feel like a convertible roof for the sake of people seeing you, more like a way of letting the world develop and enhance your experience of the car. Smell the brakes, feel the rush of air, be assaulted by the engine note. In fact, to drive this car in the blazing sun – the smells of the countryside whipping into the cabin and the engine bouncing merrily around the hills above Maranello – is nothing short of magical.

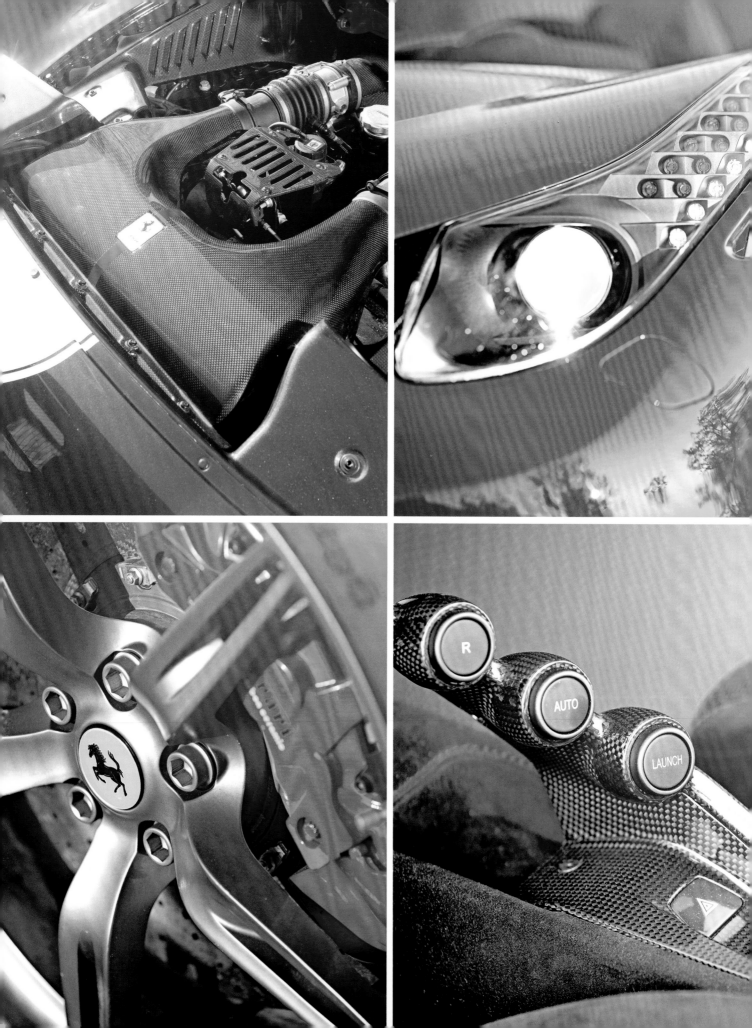

UNITED STATES OF MUSTANG

WHAT BETTER WAY TO CELEBRATE THE MUSTANG'S 50TH BIRTHDAY THAN DRIVE IT TO EVERY STATE IN AMERICA? WELL, ALMOST...

've got the windows up and the air-conditioning on full blast, but I'm still sweating like I've sprung a leak. The hot and humid air swirling around the cabin is already so saturated with moisture it can't absorb any of mine. In front of me is a quarter-mile drag strip covered in so much grip goo it's like a giant piece of flypaper. Behind and to the side of me in the grandstand is a crowd of people waiting expectantly for something historic to happen.

A big dude with an even bigger beard beckons me forward, so I slam the lever into first, hear and feel the clunk of the Torsen diff engaging, then roll slowly towards the staging line. As I do that, there's a small whine of feedback from the PA system as it spools up, then, 'Lay-deez and-ha gen-tle-men, put your hands together for the first 2015 Ford Mustang!' And, as the crowd follows the instruction, I nail the throttle, dump the clutch and lunge forward into the Carolina night on the 2015 Mustang's first ever run down a drag strip.

How do we know it's the first time? Because everything we've done so far – and will do over the next couple of weeks – is a 2015 Mustang world first. We've got Number One off the line right here, so anything we do with it – fill it with petrol, get a ticket, eat crisps, burp, anything – are all new Mustang world firsts. Which is a huge privilege, of course, but not one that was won lightly. We had to convince Ford that we had the best plan for celebrating the launch of the 2015 model, which we all now know is finally coming to the UK.

So we thought of lots of clever ideas. Then we binned

WHERE IS IT?
The big thing between Canada and Mex

WHICH BIT?
Almost all of it

GIVE ME CO-ORDINATES!
Don't you have a map?

WHEN SHOULD I GO?
This depends on how much you value your job.
Tomorrow?

HOW LONG WILL IT TAKE?
Two weeks if you go hard, two months if you're a
normal human

HOW DO I GET THERE?
You could build a rudimentary raft, but we
recommend an aeroplane

WHAT'S THE WEATHER LIKE?
Ample

WHAT'S THE ROAD LIKE?
Interstatey

WHAT IF I GET LOST?
You will end up in Vegas with a stripper in your
bathroom. Stay strong

TG TOP TIP:
Follow our wiggly route for a foolproof way to visit
every state in one swoop

ONE MORE THING:
Don't forget Hawaii. Unfortunately we missed the
boat…

all those and went with an obvious one. At the time of writing, The Mustang is 50 years old. There are 50 states in the US. Why don't we drive the car through all of them to celebrate both facts, introducing the US to its favourite pony car one state at a time? Deal, said Ford, calling our bluff and causing a major breakout of Serious Planning. Or partially serious. Associate editor Tom Ford wondered what all the fuss was about. 'Surely we just amble senselessly about America. No?'

No. Well, actually, yes. But not before a couple of months of staring at Google Maps, more travel arrangements than an evacuation and many, many logistical realisations – like just how far Alaska really is from the rest of the US. What emerged was a route that looked like the work of an over-caffeinated, ink-dipped spider. It started in Maine on the east coast and wiggled its way west to the final destination: the Sunset Marquis hotel just off Sunset Boulevard in Los Angeles, California. Total mileage? 11,175.5, as the cursor flies. Time to do it? About two weeks. Possible problems? Too many

to list. A road trip to remember? You betcha.

The central star of which we'd left to Ford to choose and specify. The sensible Mustang, in retrospect, for this long-distance, on-the-limit cruise through the US's urban and open spaces would have been a GT with the 5.0-litre V8, the comfiest seats and kindest suspension possible plus the lightest gearbox to take the sting out of all the city work, of which there was plenty.

But Ford, clearly expecting us to race every moving thing up to and including our own shadow after burning out a set of tyres before breakfast each morning, went straight to the toughest end of the options list. This gave rise to a Ruby Red GT (all GTs are V8s) fitted with a pair of Recaro race seats and the US-only Performance Pack. This includes bigger brakes, more bracing, stiffer suspension, wider 19-inch wheels and a 0.373 rear axle with, as we would be reminded with a thump every time we selected first, a Torsen diff. If we'd been on a track, we'd have wanted this spec. For our tour-athon it seemed a little harsh. So that's the set-up. Over these 36 pages, you can ride shotgun with us as we introduce ourselves, and the US as a whole, to the 2015 Mustang. Sitting

comfortably? Then we'll begin…

I didn't expect to see a tortoise. Not here in the middle of a deserted misty freeway just a few miles from Atlanta. And, to be fair, the tortoise probably wasn't expecting to see a bright red Mustang GT bearing down on him at 75mph either. But here we were, marveling momentarily at each other's unlikely presence. He travelling at 100ft a day, we moving at roughly that much per second.

No, I'm not going to flog the old hare and tortoise story, although on a journey this twisted, if he'd carried on heading due west he might well have beaten us to California. What struck me was the way we were both gazing at each other. Staring had been a common theme ever since we had picked up the Mustang three days earlier at Granite Ford in Rochester, New Hampshire. We drove around staring at people and things, and people stared back at us and pointed. They also grinned, laughed, gasped, high-fived, sang, went for their guns and generally loved being in the close proximity of this first of a new breed of Mustang.

They also, to a person, strangely seemed to know instantly what it was. Like its picture had been on the side

TOP: *Pat stops for a quick lube, and decides the car should probably have one while he's at it.*

LEFT (OPPOSITE PAGE): *Outside of the Ford dealership in Main, the shiny new Stang has no idea what's about to hit it.*

LEFT: *In less than two weeks, on the other side of America, the trip computer will tell a very different story…*

of cereal packets for weeks, or beamed into the nation's consciousness. Almost everyone – men, women and kids, many of whom we saw tugging on their parents' sleeves and pointing – saw it, knew it and loved it. If someone commits a crime and a bystander sees the getaway car in the UK, all that most people could tell you is its colour. In the US, anyone of almost any age could immediately tell you the make, model and year without blinking. Especially if it were a Mustang.

That includes Kim, who is playing with her kids on an idyllic stretch of beach at our first stop in Maine. Seeing the Mustang appear, all of them drop their buckets and spades and rush towards the car for a better look. Kim knows it's the new Stang as she coincidentally works at the local Ford dealership. Her kids 'just know, alright?' it's a new Mustang, and that's apparently enough to make them ecstatic. After crawling all over it, leaving sand everywhere and doing selfies in the passenger seat, they pronounce it 'very cool', which bodes well for the Mustang keeping its long-term appeal. If these sub millennials like it so much, maybe this 50-year-old model could see its centenary, too.

But first it has to transport us through another 18 states in less than 48 hours, so we have to get a move on. This first leg runs from Maine, the most north-easterly of US states, then wiggles down the eastern seaboard through – deep breath here – New Hampshire, Vermont, Massachusetts, New York, Rhode Island, Connecticut, New Jersey, Delaware, Maryland, Pennsylvania, Virginia, West Virginia, Ohio, Kentucky, Tennessee, North and South Carolina before screeching to a halt in Atlanta, Georgia for the next crew to take over. So it's as much about endurance as sightseeing. And because we need to bag all 19 states, we have to use our own wobbly navigation skills, not the Stang's in-built unit which would take us direct.

Or it would if it could understand our UK accents. Voice is the only way you can programme it on the move. We tried all the usual British ways of talking to foreigners – talking more slowly, then more slowly at twice the volume, then shouting – but none of them worked. We even tried talking with a rubbish American accent, which just seemed to confuse it even more. When we came to a stop and tried programming it manually, we had a chilling realisation. There aren't 50 states in

the US – there are, according to the nav, 66. Thinking that we'd blown it before we'd hardly started, we looked a bit closer and felt a little better. Being a US unit, it had been programmed with all US-owned territories, like Puerto Rico, the American Virgin Islands, Guam, American Samoa and the other 12 that have people on them. But even that's not it. Pub fact #150,965: there are another nine, such as Baker Island, which are uninhabited. So 75 in all.

But the navigation system was not our only issue. The six-speed gearbox, which we were working quite hard as we ground through the Boston, and then NYC, traffic snarl-ups, also wasn't helping matters. At first we thought it was just a bit new and tight, but after a few hundred miles it was exactly the same – awkward, heavy and noisy. Thinking there might be something wrong with it, we pinged the factory, and the message came back – no, this is how it's meant to be. The Performance Pack has been designed almost solely to make the 2015 V8 beat the outgoing 2013 Boss 302 around a track. Something that Ford assured us it does, which is impressive. But the cost

of beating the 302 is that it makes the Mustang a grumpy companion for city work.

With a lower-geared rear axle making all the ratios in the 'box shorter, first feels too low and the increased torque makes shifting harder and less precise unless you are going flat-out. Likewise, the Torsen diff is a brilliant way of making sure more of the power finds its way to the track than a regular LSD, but the pay off is it feels like the driveshaft is loose when running at road speeds.

Particularly as the rest of the car is so much better than ever before. There's the design of it for starters, which has managed to modernise all the Mustang cues without messing them up. Then there's the aero-inspired interior with its Bell & Ross watch-alike clocks, big alloy cross beam and variable drive and steering modes. There are still a few spots where the plastics could be better – like around the handbrake – but generally the fixtures and fittings are of way higher quality. And then there's the chassis, which finally ditches the solid rear axle for an independently sprung item.

The first impression this gives is that the car is heavier,

because it feels more tied down, particularly at the back. But since the weight difference in the components is only around 25kg, that's mostly an illusion. It also makes the car feel slower, as we've become used to Mustangs getting lively when the speed rises. Not so in this car, which stays composed and linear right up to, and even beyond, its limits. So it's as much about recalibrating your expectations of what a Mustang can do – and I speak as the previous owner of two classic Mustangs – as much as anything else. Ford is the master of making blue-collar cars ride and handle, and it's not dropped the ball here. This becomes ever more clear as we leave behind the big cities and head up into the Blue Ridge Mountains. Out here, despite the blanket police coverage – clearly one of the main employment opportunities – the Mustang can breathe a little better and the route becomes more of a challenge than a gridlocked chore. But, just as the fun starts, we are quickly zeroing in on our final destination for this leg.

The handover point in Atlanta, GA, is a Holiday Inn just next to the airport. We'd picked this place as it looked like the quiet sort of hotel where nothing ever happened. We couldn't have been more wrong. If it had known what was going to transpire, even the tortoise would have probably taken one look and got out of there – fast.

After a relatively smooth first stint, leg two begins with a less auspicious set of circumstances. Dan Read (and veteran co-pilot Piers Ward) take the reins...

On my last trip to the Deep South, I found myself on the wrong end of a biker's handgun. Let's just say I upset his oversized wife with ambitious overtaking, which was disciplined by a .45 pointed at my kneecaps. But all was well, and after a few diplomatic words and some hysterical pleading, he let me go so long as I promised never to return.

This time, I'm welcomed by the sight of a dead teenager, pulled from a hotel pool after a drinking session ended up in the deep end. They wheel him through the lobby on a paramedic's trolley, all damp and limp like a supermarket fish. I should've learned. It might have been a few years since I was around these parts, but the mood hasn't changed much. And it doesn't get much brighter when we eventually hit the road...

Indeed, if you were to judge the South by the roadside

peckish, your roadkill barbecue would contain choice cuts of armadillo, turtle breasts and perhaps a side of raccoon paw.

Next, it's history's shortest visit to Florida before nipping across Mississippi and into Louisiana, where everything above sea level is on stilts, including the road. They put up little green signs that tell you what's below, most of which inspire you to drive as fast as possible to the next state line. Because while the frontiersmen to the north-west named their places with cheerful optimism, the southern settlers took a more literal approach. Murder Creek. Gashland. Turkey Foot. In fact, according to some roadside literature – spelled out letter by letter on *Countdown*-style squares outside churches – the only hope in these parts is that Jesus will return to sort things out. Probably from a southerly direction, skiing barefoot over a bayou with a smoke on the go. Feeling safe in that knowledge, we hit the outskirts of New Orleans and drive the Mustang to a levee, but it didn't rhyme… so we left. We do the rest of Louisiana in darkness, which is probably for the best. Heading north-west on I49 we make a quick pit stop near the town of Alexandria (turns out three minutes is plenty of time to be attacked by a plague of randy locusts) before an overnight stop in Texarkana, which straddles two states. Ten points if you can guess which ones. That's six states down today, 25 in total, and 25 to go. Each of which will have its flag glued to the Stang's fuselage in the style of an old bomber's mission markings.

On Monday morning, the clammy swamps give way to cattle ranches as we touch upon cowboy country. The temperature has dropped from a hundred degrees to a more comfortable 80ish, and the Mustang is gulping down the morning air as if it were a strawberry smoothie. Yes, you can have it in Europe with a four-cylinder engine and that's all very sensible, but – let's be honest – you can't beat the lazy churning of a big V8. Out here in its homeland, anything else just wouldn't feel right. It's actually quite comforting knowing it's up there, all five litres, stirring its pistons for mile after mile like a ship at sea. At least the petrol's cheap, mostly because it's awful low-octane stuff that explodes in the cylinders with the fury of a party popper.

This morning shall mostly be spent in Arkansas, which of course is famous for Bill Clinton and… that's about

it. It's an attractive place with surprisingly deep, wooded valleys that cradle red barns and tidy farmhouses straight from Sylvanian Families. Those shouty billboards have thinned out, and middle America is looking like a more pleasant land, after all. We're off the interstate for a bit, sweeping through the hills, where the road occasionally bends to resemble a very mild corner.

Left into Oklahoma. Up into Kansas and a quick right towards Joplin, Missouri, where we pick up the old Route 66 for a while. Back in the day, this is where you'd have found real America, in the rail-car diners and pink motels serving road-trippers as they zipped around the highways in chromed Hudsons and Studebakers. It's very tempting to add the good ol' Mustang to that list, but it arrived much later in '64, by which time Eisenhower's interstates had begun slicing up the landscape and, with it, American road culture itself. You can still piece together the old route, but it's now mostly four-lane freeway that starves the towns the Mother Road once fed.

Indeed, our Stang is doing a fairly good job of shrinking this big old place. Just yesterday morning we were rolling out of Atlanta, now here we are driving north-east across Missouri, which is serving up the mother of all thunderstorms. The sky pulses with the electric whites and purples of a warehouse rave, and great sheets of light turn the nightscape briefly into green fields and golden bales. Then comes the rain and the spray as the trucks roar past, and the only way to keep a straight line is to thump the cat's eyes. We cross into Illinois, the car seems happy enough; its human contents, less so. Time for bed.

We awake on Day Three in Terre Haute, Indiana, home of Ron Burgundy and – perhaps more interestingly – just a short drive, by American standards, from Indianapolis Motor Speedway. An old lady with a puff of white hair waves us merrily through the gates where we take some pictures and spread the map over the hood. Would've been nice to do a lap of the oval, but there isn't time. Instead, let's divert 180 miles north for a brief stop at the Mustang's birthplace, Michigan, where the sober messages of the South are replaced by ads for sex and gambling emporiums – separate establishments, although the billboards suggest otherwise (Buffalo Ben Casinos: The Loosest Slots in Town!) We've come a long way…

Plenty of miles to do, though. Before bed today we'll be stuck in Chicago traffic, misplace a credit card at a gas station – doubling back 30 miles and a timezone to retrieve it – and cross Wisconsin and Minnesota, both of which look like autumnal Oxfordshire, if autumnal Oxfordshire had skunks and Harley-Davidsons.

Day Four. North and South Dakota? Pretty much in Canada. Grassy. Occasional bison. Heading due south now and across another state line to Iowa. The author Bill Bryson once wrote: 'I come from Des Moines. Somebody had to,' and although we're some way west of his hometown, you can see his point. So my notepad takes an extended break before we cross the border to Nebraska, where, if your dog ran off, you could see it for three days. (I might have fast-forwarded a bit here – it actually takes the best part of 10 hours to cover the miles described in this paragraph, but let's just say I saved you the trouble).

We overnight in Grand Island, which is neither grand, nor an island. But it was the location for an exciting series of tornadoes that swept through town in June 1980, on what was dubbed the Night of the Twisters. Six people were carried away and 200 more were hurt, while those who made it to shelters emerged to find their houses on different streets. As a memorial to the souls who were blown away, they piled the debris in a park outside town and called it Tornado Hill. There's no plaque. So in quiet contemplation, we head off in search of a nice breakfast and a way back to the laser-straight I80 for the final run to Denver.

Not only does I80 – otherwise known as the Lincoln Highway – trace the first transcontinental road across America, but this part also follows the Oregon Trail, an old pioneer's route from east to west. Thousands of wagons once came this way, following one after the other through ruts so deep they're actually still here, carved out of the chalky riverbanks that run alongside the modern road. Crossing America back then was a more dangerous business. This wasn't the wildest part of the west, but if the bandits and Indians didn't get you, the freezing winters probably would.

This may explain the historic job advert we find in a well-preserved Pony Express station just off the freeway near Gothenburg. 'Wanted: young, wiry fellows. Must be expert riders and prepared to risk death daily. Orphans preferred.' The successful candidate would become a

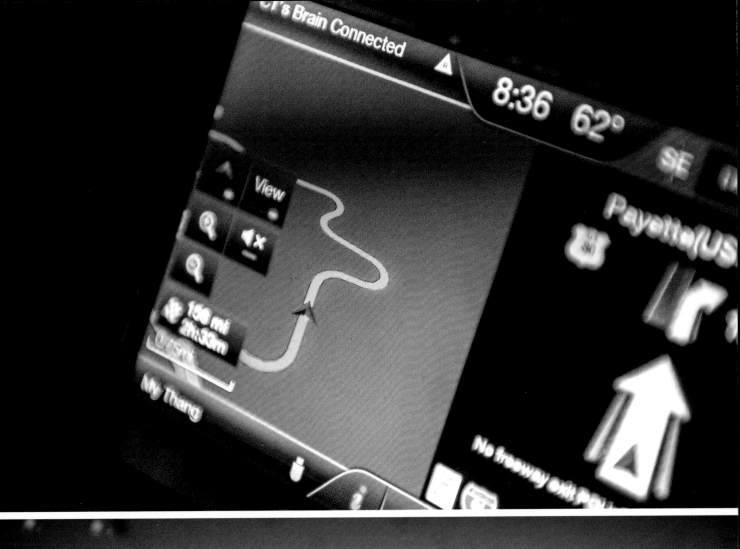

postman on horseback, responsible for carrying mail and messages from east to west as quickly as possible. The best of them would cover over 100 miles a day, stopping at a wooden station every 10 miles to swap horses. While they used all sorts of tame thoroughbreds, for a really fast blast across these lonely plains there was only one suitable steed. A wild Mustang.

With horses doing the hard miles, news had never travelled so fast in America, but despite heroic efforts – and with a team of riders including Buffalo Bill – the whole endeavour lasted only 18 months, when the men and ponies proved too costly and were eventually replaced by telegraph wires.

How things have changed, eh? Our Mustang has so far travelled a whopping 5,360 miles in seven days and only demanded a drink or two. While it's good to go for a while longer, these particular riders are a bit saddle-sore. So it's a relief when – on a dusty road linking Wyoming to Colorado – we approach a figure on the horizon. Looking like some sort of hairless hitchhiker, our very own Ollie Marriage has turned up as promised, and will take things from here. So from this crew, it's over and out. For you, the journey continues...

With the Midwest done and dusted, Ollie Marriage takes over as the Mustang's epic adventure heads up and over the Rockies, then across the deserts beyond...

Ha, bloody ha, Dan. I thought I'd heard chortling in the background when they'd asked me to meet them at the junction of Jefferson Avenue and Iris Hills Lane ('it's only a bit north of Denver…'), and alarm bells should have rung when my taxi driver looked positively gleeful when I informed him I wanted to go to 'a suburb called Wellington, it's a bit north'.

Some 90 minutes later I'm standing at a crossroads on a dirt track in the precise middle of nowhere, Colorado, $100 lighter and cursing my colleagues. They turn up, grinning like the berks they are, but not grinning quite so widely when, handover complete, I drive off, leaving them with no more than their bags and the number of a taxi firm. It wouldn't have been right to subject them to the tyranny of the back seat a moment longer.

So now it's just photographer Justin and I and a couple

of hundred miles of Colorado before the next sleep and beyond that, mountains, desert, salt, two types of tyre damage, more mountains, forest and finally the Pacific Ocean. Two thousand two hundred miles lie ahead, and it's a hell of a lot more varied than the territory encountered by the plainsmen who have just exited the Stang. It's now Thursday evening; we have to be in Seattle by Sunday lunchtime. Back through Denver, hang a right, tune radio to Godrock FM (the message of the Lord through the medium of metal…) and drive straight at the Rockies that loom ahead, darker through the broad windscreen than the inky sky. Denver's already a mile high, and the Grand Army of the Republic highway (aka I70) takes a suitably military approach, spearing upwards along the path of least resistance to the highest point the Stang'll hit on the entire, massive 50-state extravaganza – an Alpine pinnacle-matching 3,496 metres.

For neither the first nor last time, the Mustang crosses the Continental Divide. I already like this big coupé for its vastly improved ride quality and lazy, easy mile-covering ability, but it is struggling on these high-topped hills. A combination of long gearing and altitude is robbing breath from the Mustang's lungs and forcing regular downchanges. Hadn't expected that. And when you do downshift, it's not like you're accessing rolling exhaust thunder – for a thumping V8, it's a bit tame.

We overnight in the upmarket ski town of Vail, dining on a takeout Chinese in the Holiday Inn's darkened timber lobby. We calculate we need to do over 900 miles tomorrow. Hell's teeth.

By 7am, we've already done nearly 100 miles, passed signs for Bellyache Ridge, Blowout Hill and No Name, dived through a gorge alongside the Colorado River and found ourselves vainly chasing a dawn sun around Carbondale. It's a cool mountain town, rustically fashionable, the kind of place where it's impossible to spot a Subaru without a bike rack. That becomes our Colorado challenge. We succeed twice.

We're off the interstate now, and I've got itchy throttle leg. Not because I want to see what the Stang can do, rather because 250 miles of B-road is going to play havoc with our average speed. Route 133 is not only stunning, but also fortunately empty, wide, sweepy and rapid. The independent rear suspension has transformed this car. Gone is the back axle skitter-skatter, while the front end

aims itself obligingly – it's stable, secure and more pleasing than I expected. We crest passes, flow with silvery rivers and 243 miles of foresty, mountainy goodness later, we emerge into a very different landscape at Cortez. The wholesome-mountain-to-bare-desert transition happens shockingly quickly. Green fades to yellow, yellow to brown, and as the colours dry up, everything fades away: vegetation, towns, life. All that's left is a road, and then just off the 160, a place called Four Corners: Colorado, New Mexico, Arizona and Utah.

It surprised me to learn that this is the only place in America where four states meet, but in terms of sticker efficiency, it's great. We drive down to the collection of cubicles flogging tourist tat that surround 'The Spot' that Colorado butts up against New Mexico, Arizona and Utah. I play solo Twister across four states and then contemplate how feasible it would be to drift the Mustang round the outside of the whole complex. Very feasible. But likely to end with four kinds of state troopers taking umbrage.

New Mexico: in a state that measures maybe 300 miles north to south, we do about 750 metres. Amazingly, it looks very similar to Colorado and then… Arizona: after 39 empty miles relieved only by a health centre and a school, both notable mainly for their incongruity in this sun-blasted place, we flick back north and cross into… Utah. Utah is clearly rather proud of itself. The sign welcoming us ('Life Elevated') is big and colourful, the smaller sign next to it informing us we are still 1,634 metres above sea level (we won't drop below 600m of altitude until the final run into Seattle).

Gutting though it is, we simply don't have time to chase rainbows on this trip. I look out the driver's window and can see the bastions of Monument Valley edging past, 20 miles west. I point it out to Justin, who tells me of his disappointment when Dan refused to divert to Little House on the Prairie. A gloom settles on the car, that only lifts when we spot some lonely horses out across the scrubby desert. Must be mustangs.

There's a dirt track, so I spear off for a closer look, towing a healthy cloud of dust. Whereupon they leg it, and we're alone in an even more lonely bit of desert. And unable to see where we're going until the dust clears.

Next stop is Arches National Park. There are two decent

towns in the 130 miles between here and there. Two towns and a million Hollywood clichés. But those clichés are just life occurring out here. Big bearded men do ride Harleys, trucks do honk at each other, tumbleweed does blow and the blacktop does run laser-straight.

No one bats an eyelid at the Mustang. It only gets recognised as being the 'twenny-fideen' car twice on our stint. People are interested in the stickers though, so we tell them what we're up to, and they just think that's cool. Imagine telling your average Brit you were driving around the UK touching every county – they'd think you were barking. But Americans are open and accepting, less judgemental, and that runs through their whole attitude to cars and how they use them. It's why road-tripping out here is so good.

As the sun lowers, we conduct a whistle-stop tour of the Arches National Park. For an hour, our minds are bent by the shapes wrought by wind, water and sandstone. Then we realise it's 7.30pm and we have the small matter of 350 miles to do before shut-eye.

Driving the Mustang is like receiving a warm, reassuring hug. The large Recaro seats are beyond perfection for their expansive support and comfort, and it smashes great distances to smithereens. It does so now, as the sun drops out of sight and we finally, for the first time since it rose this morning, get on a multi-lane road. And then off it again. Another 125 miles of unlit single-lane stuff. Towns pass, time passes, the treeless scenery is constant. We keep rolling along. The Mustang is a metronome and will do 320–350 miles between fills, the occupants somewhat less hardy. The motor hums, hours are consumed, in the temporary flash of bright lights that is Salt Lake City, we glimpse the Mormon Temple. Then, at around midnight, I lose my perspective. Red and blue lights flash ahead through the featurelessness of the crystal-clear night, so I back off immediately. It takes six miles to reach the cop car. Relief and exhaustion wash over me when we pull into Wendover at 1am.

And out at 5.30am. With good reason: dawn on Bonneville Salt Flats. I've been wanting to come here for a dose of salt fever for so long, and I'm mesmerised. It's the colour, texture and scale of the place, soft blues and lilacs tinging the distant dawn mountains. The gentle burble of V8s is lost across the miles of whitening salt as

the Utah Salt Flats Racing Association early birds crawl out through the puddles in search of dry salt. Bonneville is a cultural, as well as natural, wonder.

Skirting close to Nevada, we pick up Route 30, my favourite road on the whole trip. In 70 miles, we see four cars, a tree hung with bottles and one vast train whose haunting horn echoes across the valley. We cruise alongside it, then zap ahead and stop at the crossing. The bell rings, and we stand as close as we dare (not very) as the leviathan thunders by, a couple of unprotected metres away. It's a rush. Yee-hawing and caught up in the road-trip vibe, we stop and do a burnout on what turns out to be a phenomenally abrasive road surface. We've lunched the tyres, which calms us down quite effectively.

Utah is a cool state, has an extrovert gene and is chock-full of people having fun in the wacky landscapes. Idaho is its polar opposite. Life Elevated gives way to Potato State. The territory here has been cultivated, agriculture has tamed the wildness, there's irrigation, and regular towns that all morph into one. You know how Scooby Doo runs through a house and every third door is a repeat? That's Idaho. Groundhog scenery. It's interminable, but at least the authorities allow you to hurry through it – the interstate limit is 80mph.

Montana: this, photographer Justin and I decide, is our favourite state. We even like the bus graveyard just east of the state line on I15. To be honest, we find ourselves occasionally wishing that Americans would clean up after themselves a bit better. No rural homestead anywhere seems to be complete without the wreck of a half-rotted pickup in the yard. But Montana is a majestic place that wears man's intrusion lightly. There's something reassuring about this lofty state in its stillness and tranquillity. Like the Scottish Highlands, there's a sense of ancient calmness. The peaks are proud and solid, the hillsides blanketed with velvety grasslands, the air warm and fresh. It's both wild and welcoming. I90 swings west after Butte, there's a very twisty-turny bit when we run alongside the Clark Fork River which the Mustang is more than a match for, the sun sets, then a two-foot section of tyre tread flicks up from the car in front and crashes through the front foglight. No harm done. We pass back through Idaho (it's a weird shape) and finally cross into our final state.

Washington: just the 16 hours and 830 miles in the car

today, to add to the 19 hours and 920 miles yesterday. Pooped, we hole up for the night in Spokane. Washington then catches us by surprise the next morning by being a repeat of Idaho. We'd thought Pacific north-west, tall trees, mountains and piney goodness, but that's all tucked into a narrow band by the coast. Apart from a zone of interest around the Columbia River Gorge, Washington only gets interesting when snow-bound Mount Rainier puts in an appearance.

From there it's a gorgeous run into Seattle on a sparkling Sunday. Green, wealthy and welcoming, Seattle is a sunny Scandinavia of a place. We come in on the Alaskan Way Viaduct, waterfront on our left, skyscrapers high to the right, and promptly get lost when the on-board satnav lets us down for the first time in 2,140 miles. But our destination isn't hard to find, 'Just look for *The Jetsons'* skyscraper,' Tom had said. We find him and editor Charlie in the shadow of the Space Needle. Ten minutes later, the Mustang rounds a corner and disappears. I feel forlorn. Justin, who's called it home for more than a week, looks empty. We find a bar. Above it hangs a T-shirt that reads 'Step aside coffee, this is a job for whisky.' Now's the time.

The greatest distance for the fewest amount of states. Tom Ford and Charlie Turner leave America in search of another bit of... America

Turns out that the first thing you notice, when settling into the cabin of a car that's been occupied solely by adult males non-stop for the past few hundred hours, is the smell. The kind of latent musk that seeps from pores fed with a drive-by diet and watered by sticky caffeine sweats means that this Mustang is not somewhere I'd like to put someone with a fragile immune system. Because they would die. The outside is much the same, now a scuffed and muted ruby, the front scarred with legion insectile suicides and the passenger's side plastered with stickers from every state – a graphic diary of success and inexorable, grinding distance. There aren't many places left to fill: 45 flags already decorate the Stang's flank. But we're nowhere near done. America is – as we have been discovering – really quite distressingly big, and to tick off the next in the series, most of our road miles won't even be in the USA. Charlie and I will be driving all the

way through British Columbia in Canada to the US state of Alaska. And then back down the same road to Las Vegas, Nevada, via Oregon. With no time to waste, we salute Ollie and Justin, and head out from the shadow of Seattle's Space Needle. We've got a ferry to catch, and exactly 1,001.5 miles between us and it.

It's good to get going. The Stang still feels strong and vital despite the abuse it's probably suffered in the hands of most of the *TopGear* office up to this point. Yes, the clutch and 'box are probably more vintage than they were just a scant few days ago – and that diff thumps like a truck – but the interior is holding up impeccably, and the engine purrs away up front like it's just getting into its stride. Unfortunately, we aren't getting into ours – Seattle traffic means we spend the first couple of hours of our journey heading north staring at an endless sea of crimson brakelights. It's 3pm.

We track north out of Washington State on I5, burbling gently through Mount Vernon and Bellingham before striking out on minor roads to hit the smaller Canadian border at Sumas, a tactic we thought might save some time. It doesn't, and we grind to a halt in border traffic for nearly two hours. After a chafingly dull wait, Charlie turns his ineffable charm on the female border guard, inevitably leading to us being hauled up for a detailed search and interview. This bit doesn't go well.

'Is it a coincidence that your name is Tom Ford and you're driving a Ford car from Ford Motor Company?' asks the customs officer suspiciously, managing to look in two directions simultaneously.

'Well, I'm not an incredibly wealthy gay fashion icon!' I blurt. The customs officer looks confused, and then a bit angry. We are delayed further.

Eventually, among a furrow of suspicious looks and a surprisingly coquettish smile from a burly uniform, we are released into Canada and turn right onto the Trans-Canada Highway. We run through Chilliwack and turn leftish at the town of Hope, before relaxing and settling into a mile-eating lope, but despite the Stang's obvious abilities in the marathon sphere, we aren't going to get as far as we hoped. Charlie books us a hotel 'not too far away', and not one of those 'nasty chain hotels'. I trust him. Four and a half hours later and a fuel stop away, we are driving down a dirt road somewhere north of a place called 100-Mile House, in the pitch black, slaloming cows.

'Cow,' intones Charlie as we slither around a huge black bovine shape lying in the carriageway, as if identifying that it is not, in fact, a dragon. It's getting creepy, we're deep in a BC forest, and the hotel is, according to the directions, some 15km from the nearest road. Phones have stopped working, but it's late, we're out of options, and we need to sleep. We roll into a ranch, lit by the soft, warm glow of 40-watt bulbs, and a lovely lady called Myrna ushers us into a small log cabin with bunk beds. We can just make out the glittery expanse of a lake a few hundred yards away, and the cabin is warm and smells of pine. Exhausted, pleased that we're not going to be murdered by banjo-wielding woodsmen, it feels like heaven as we fall into bed. Early next morning, it turns out that it doesn't just feel like heaven.

It actually is.

John and Myrna Barkowsky have run this place, called Spring Lake Ranch, for over three decades. It's a place you can rent a cabin, but also used to, and sometimes still does, function as a refuge for troubled teens. It's also idyllic enough to make your teeth ache. It sits on a goodly expanse of picture-perfect lake, and there are ducks and eagles and horses and deer. The ranch cats are as attentive as spaniels, and if you leave a Mustang still for long enough, John will brand it. As we discovered. Apparently, anything bearing his mark, he technically owns – a practical joke followed by the kind of generous laugh that makes Father Christmas seem like a withered old curmudgeon. Myrna cooks us breakfast, and we head off a whole lot brighter than when we started. But we have to go. The road does not wait.

Next up is a place called Terrace. It's supposed to be an easy 600ish-mile, 12-hour stint, but turns into much more, mainly because of logging trucks, low speed limits and scenery that causes you to involuntarily slow down, just to take it all in. There's not exactly much to do for a passenger: navigation consists of hooking one left from the '97 onto the I16 at a small town called Prince George and tracking the scenery. There is a lot of scenery. Gorges with wide rivers looping through the bottoms, capped with the dancing froth of whitewater rapids. Many, many trees – mainly spruce and cedar and northern hemlock – ranked and endless, and unnamed mountains stoic against a steel-grey sky. We track through Houston and Smithers, stopping to look at the world's largest fly-fishing rod (surprisingly big, joyously pointless), past the Babine Mountains and Seven Sisters. Every corner brings a fresh, horizon-wide vista, and there are no big towns – just little hamlets, utilitarian and haphazard. It's a beautiful, wild place, even now, but even though you start the day awed, the scale and beauty is a little eroded by the sheer expanse and endlessness of the drive. Imagine the Highlands of Scotland to 200 per cent scale, and then stretched over one hundred times the area. After a couple of days, you tend to want to see something other than a tree.

We sleep in Terrace, which turns out to be a practical, unpretentious town, and then head to Prince Rupert the next morning. It's an easy drive, but as we near the coast, the mist rolls in and lurks in unlikely places, making it feel more than a little spooky. At one point, the road dips and then rises in the distance on a long straight – and simply disappears from bright sunshine into a vague opaque blur. Like driving past the edge of reality. We arrive in PR, and wait for the ferry across the bottom curve of the Gulf of Alaska to Ketchikan – we will next see land in our first sticker-state. More waiting, then through the US border control – we're heading back into United States territory, so I force Turner into silence with a few sharp prods – and then we're on the boat, along with just five other cars and 24 other people, on a ferry that can cope with 750. It means there are few witnesses to what happens next, when the humpback whales start leaping out of the water and slapping their immense tails against the sea not 100ft from the boat. We can see that this is a sizeable pod from the blowhole spume trails, but several adults are showing off, leaping about like animate rocky islands. It's humbling to see, though I keep expecting David Attenborough's voice to murmur explanations. It's a bit disappointing when it never happens.

We arrive in Ketchikan, on Revillagigedo Island on the southern portion of Alaska's – ahem – 'Inside Passage' region at night, and apply our singular sticker from the past 1,500 miles. It feels like a frontier, even now. Possibly a little touristy – the main sources of income these days are commercial fishing and the wallet-lightening of cruise liners – but small and pretty and exciting. A staging post for adventures. Next morning, and at a loose end until the ferry back in the evening, we decide to visit Gravina Island in the Alexander Archipelago, upon which is built Ketchikan's local, decent-sized airport. Unfortunately, due to some rather haphazard planning, the bridge that was supposed to connect the Revillagigedo 'mainland' never got built, seeing as it would have restricted access to the financially important mega ships. So the airport is isolated a five-minute ferry ride

away, surrounded by a half-formed and then hastily aborted road network. Basically, Gravina is like a giant rally stage – huge, wide gravel roads through ancient, stunted forests, with roads that simply… stop. The Mustang is most excellent fun here, mainly because it's a 5.0-litre, rear-wheel-drive Mustang on deserted gravel roads. There may have been incidences of stonechips. There were certainly incidences of sideways. Almost worth the trip on its own.

After playing for a while, we seek out some of Ketchikan's usual domestic transport – floatplanes. There are hundreds of these pontoon-pointed seaplanes constantly buzzing overhead – used like taxis and entirely common – but to an Englishman, utterly romantic. Charlie seriously considers a change of career to piloting a De Havilland DHC-2 Beaver, and then revises his opinion when informed of the danger. It reinforces the notion that we are on the edge of an expanse – where the only way to get where you want to go from this point on takes more than a car. Appropriate: the Tongass National Forest to the north stretches to a place called Yakutat Bay for *17 million* acres. Back to the mainland, and a few hours before the ferry back, we drive around the bottom of Alaska, through Alice-in-Wonderland chromium-green forests, marvelling at rivers full of salmon. Until that is, you realise that they are all dying after spawning, and the entire place stinks to high heaven of rotting fish. Attenborough's dulcet tones again fail to make an appearance, so we head back to the ferry.

The boat back to Canada takes a while. It is glass calm on the water, and no lights to see, other than those we bring. If I didn't know better, it would feel like we were on a spaceship, gliding through the void. There are bunkbeds again and no windows. The less said about that, the better. A repeat of the America/Canada border for a few hours, and then the cold, hard realisation of what's been in the back of our minds all along – we are about to reprise the entire journey, a day later. Pat Devereux happily texts us to joke that to get to our rendezvous in Nevada in time, we will have to average some 40mph, even when asleep. It doesn't help. What follows is a gravelly eyed lesson in déjà vu. Back down through Prince Rupert and Terrace, Prince George and the rest. We are making progress, the Mustang howling down through the gorges day and night, feeling like a low-flying aeroplane. The big, sweeping curves suit it, the speeds brisk but safe, just how the V8 likes to play. You can feel the independent rear suspension soaking up bumps that would have disturbed the previous model, and there's a new fluency to the way this one carves, but with this heavy 5.0-litre – there's a lighter four-cylinder with 300+bhp for Europe – it feels like an evolved Mustang rather than a revolution. Still, a V8 Mustang on these roads is exactly what's called for. Fitness for purpose. Eventually we make it to the US border, back at Sumas, after a blur of road and the barely touched blandness of roadside motels. We sail through the border in 10 minutes – a shock – and note that in 2,500-odd miles, we have added but one sticker to the Mustang's tally.

We whip down through Washington, clipping Oregon on the I84 for another state, eventually stopping in Ontario just outside Idaho. At some point during the evening, I allowed Turner to drive, which resulted in us having a roadside conversation with a very polite policeman at around 11pm. This would be, in the entirety of the trip, the only traffic stop, and the first ever for a 2015 Mustang. Bleak looks were exchanged. Next day encompassed Idaho, turning due south at Twin Falls and heading into Nevada (our 48th state), where the land slides gently into the desert and we briefly detoured to the Extraterrestrial Highway on the 375, looking for aliens. We found none, though there were a couple of flashes of white, just in the edges of our vision – but, then, we were a bit tired. The rest can be encompassed in the halo of two Stang headlights, a flat parabola of vision that lit nothing but highway. A time-lapse of life that ticked off the twin axes of time and distance. Right up until Las Vegas popped up out of the desert like a vomitous neon fountain, and I knew we were nearly finished.

After so much contemplation of nature, Vegas, with its fizzing, fluorescent heartbeat and endless wash of all-consuming humanity, is a shock. Strip clubs and gambling. Mega hotels and plastic. Life and death in the course of a weekend. We celebrate our epic stint to bag the fewest states by having a quiet few drinks. Unfortunately, the drink in question is Mescal and, like many lost weekends, the ensuing unquiet chaos is best never, ever spoken of again. Next morning, we meet a staunchly sober Pat, and send him on his way for the short drive to California, and the final stage of our United States of Mustang. Good luck, Pat. You get the glory ride home. You just need to make it to the finish line now. No pressure.

The final leg: Pat Devereux takes us home…

10,840 miles ago, I picked up the Stang not knowing if we'd even get to this point. You think we've forgotten, don't you? Well, we haven't. Yes, the final destination of LA is just a couple of tanks of gas away, but we still need to find a way to get to Hawaii. We said the plan was to do all 50 states, to celebrate the Mustang's 50th birthday, and we still have every intention of making that happen. Every intention, d'ya hear? The only small problem is we haven't yet quite worked out how. But there's no rush, for once. By burning time and rubber so furiously for the past couple of weeks, the crew has made up more than a day's worth of time. So we decide to take the scenic route towards Los Angeles while we make a plan. In the glittering, Brylcreemed sixties, the Rat Pack of Frank Sinatra, Dean Martin and Sammy Davis Jr would wrap up their shows in Vegas then sashay off into the desert-bound for Palm Springs for their traditional post-show party in the basement of the Caliente Tropics Hotel.

Rather than take the government-monitored freeway, they took another route across country. So we did, too. It's fair to say that the party-hungry Rat Packers didn't hang around. So neither did we. Despite owning a raft of huge, questionably styled American barges – Dean Martin had a rare Dual-Ghia Coupé, Sammy Davis got around in a 1935 Duesenberg SSJ replica, and big Frank had a penchant for Jags in his later years – Sinatra also had a taste for supercar-level speed in the form of an orange Lamborghini Miura, with orange carpets. No such styling taste issues in the Mustang. Despite more than an average year's worth of use and abuse, it still feels as strong and true as the day I picked it up in New Hampshire. The New Car Smell is long gone, as Tom says, replaced by Eau de Teenager's Fetid Bedroom, but mechanically the car's still as eager and good to go as ever. We can't go as fast as we'd like, thanks to the ever-present laser-eyed arm of the law. But we can steer as quickly as we want, which, now we've got up into the hills above Palm Springs, is turning out to be a revelation.

The last time we were up here in a GT500 and Fiesta ST, the old Stang was having trouble staying between the kerbs, the back end squirming around like a room full of preschoolers. This one is a picture of handling calm. True, as Ollie noted, sixth gear is way too long for anything other than fuel-saving cruising, even with the low-geared rear axle, but second to fifth gives you more than enough choices to row it along at speed. Just don't get me started on that noisy Torsen diff.

After a hard day of trying to rub the tread off the tyres and reduce the brake discs to wafers, we stopped at Roy's Hawaiian restaurant in Palm Desert in the vain hope it might give us some inspiration on how to get to the volcanic islands 2,500 miles away. Then, in a flicker of tiki flame, it hit us. If we just simply ignored the deadline, stuck the car on the boat for a week or two, and then brought it back a lot later, we could easily bag our 50th state and the story would be complete. Ford wouldn't miss our car – it had 49 others in LA to let other people drive. And even if it did, well, it's always better to ask for forgiveness than permission…

With that plan voted on, seconded and passed unanimously by our crew of two, early the next morning we casually checked the shipping times and had an immediate, chilling realisation – the next and only container ship to Hawaii in the next week was leaving Long Beach in two hours' time. Journey time from Palm Springs to Long Beach? Two hours fifteen on a good day. Cue a cartoonish three-second blur of doors opening, closing, engine starting and wheelspin, followed by two hours of white-knuckle, adrenaline-drenched traffic dodging on the way into LA.

'That's it!' says photographer Rowan, pointing at the harbour as we crest the hill into Long Beach. 'Which one?' I say, seeing 50 identical ships. All are about a mile away as the crow flies but we have to navigate 20 traffic junctions to get there. With 10 minutes to go, in true *Gone in 60 Seconds* style, we launch the Stang down the hill, over the bridge and scream towards the dock. Or where we think the dock is. The place is so big – it's the biggest commercial port in the world – it's hard to know for sure. I'll jump this damn thing onto the boat if I have to. We Must Make It.

But as we round the final corner to the dock, it's crushingly clear that that ain't going to happen. Our last hope of getting to Hawaii is edging slowly away from the dock on its journey west towards the US's 50th state. So we are left to watch it and our hopes disappear slowly from view. But, as horribly disappointing as it felt at that moment, the feeling didn't last long.

OK, so we didn't make it to all 50 states, but during the last 11,175.50 miles, we hit 49. Rest assured there are plans afoot to take care of this little piece of unfinished business. You didn't think we'd let this go, did you?

FORBIDDEN PLANET

IN THEORY, YOU SHOULDN'T DRIVE UP AN ERUPTING VOLCANO DURING AN EARTHQUAKE... BUT WE HAD A FIAT PANDA 4X4 HANDY, SO WE DID

When things smoke, it is usually an indication that something unfortunate is imminent. In fact, there are great swathes of things regarded with more affection when they have not recently been, or are possibly about to be, a little bit on fire. The engine in your car, for instance. Or most types of food. Unclaimed packages in airports. And mountains. Mountains are generally high on the list of things to avoid when they start to do something as uncharacteristic as lightly smoulder. But this being *TopGear*, I am currently at the base of a mountain frothing great gouts of smoke and steam, preparing to drive to the top. If the health and safety people are reading this, then I couldn't find the appropriate form. Honest.

The hell-hill in question is Mount Etna, in south-easternish Sicily, one of the most active volcanos in the world. A volcano so animate that if you tot up the major eruptions of the 20th century, they number in double figures. There are 'events' every few months. One occurred just *last night*, accompanied by a modest geological cough that measured 3.8 on the Richter scale. So today – obviously – we are going to try driving up it. Something usually forbidden, because it's a bit dangerous. For this, we require an adventure vehicle equipped with huge tyres and a massive engine, a behemoth festooned with winches and ropes and possibly anti-volcano armour. Something to protect us in case the mountain burns down. Again.

Unfortunately, we have not brought that vehicle. Instead, we have arrived equipped with a completely standard Fiat Panda 4x4. Though we have fitted winter tyres, there's a

WHERE IS IT?
Sicily

WHICH BIT?
From Catania to the crater

GIVE ME CO-ORDINATES!
37.732930, 15.007118

WHEN SHOULD I GO?
Volcanic activity has halved since 1972, so now's as good a time as any…

HOW LONG WILL IT TAKE?
Plan for a day trip

HOW DO I GET THERE?
Flights to Palermo are regular and reasonably priced. You can even hire a Panda at the airport

WHAT'S THE WEATHER LIKE?
Ashy

WHAT'S THE ROAD LIKE?
Molten

WHAT IF I GET LOST?
This is Europe's tallest active volcano, so get your escape route sorted…

TG TOP TIP:
Book a room at the Rifugio Sapienza – it's staffed by people who know a thing or two about eruptions

ONE MORE THING:
Not even the toughest tour buses can make it to the very top, but a guide will take you on foot

---

nagging feeling we may have arrived ever-so-slightly ill-equipped for this little expedition.

The situation does not bode particularly well on the drive up. Etna – all 10,922 feet of it – dominates the totality of the view that isn't sea from the town of Catania. And it's hard to miss, because it's the hill smoking like a recently fired cannon, or the remnants of the biggest firework you've ever seen. Which, in a sense, it is, because Etna is a vigorous stratovolcano two and a half times the size of Vesuvius. It's famous for featuring in Greek mythology as the place where Typhon (comfortingly called 'father of all monsters') was imprisoned by Zeus for being naughty, somewhere in an annexe to the forges of Hephaestus, the blacksmith of the gods, which are also apparently secreted under Etna's 459-square-mile base.

Sounds scary, but the bottom bit is simply pretty. Across the plain of Catania in the shadow of Etna spreads a patchwork of orchards and vineyards, rooted in the fertile volcanic soil left over from previous eruptions. It's surprisingly green, and the Panda slips into the bucolic scene as if made for it. As Etna swells in the windscreen, the bulbous little Fiat tackles the sweeping, newly laid mountain roads without fuss, little 1.3-litre MultiJet diesel thrumming through a five-speed manual. It might not be exactly crisp in its reactions, and understeer is close at hand, thanks to a couple of inches of increased height over the standard car, but the ride is supple and mature for a supermini, the body tempted into tilt but never loose. On the wet leaves and remnants of an icy dawn that

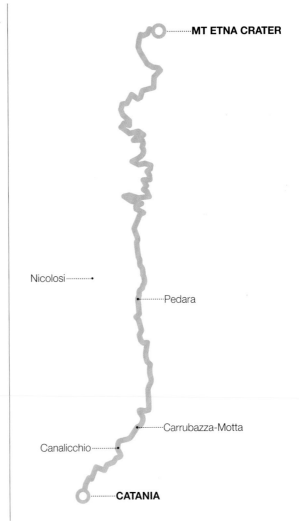

MT ETNA CRATER

Nicolosi

Pedara

Carrubazza-Motta

Canalicchio

CATANIA

shroud the bottom of the mountain, it even flickers its 4x4 system into life and drags itself out of frosty junctions without spinning wheels. This, one would suggest, is probably all that most owners would come to expect – a degree of extra surety in slippery conditions. But it looks as if we'll need a bit more than that. As if to prove some sort of meteorological point, it immediately begins to rain.

Above the forest, gently catching its own kind of fire as autumn marches its colours through the trees, old lava becomes more obvious. Spiky and yellow-green, it makes the landscape look austere and alien. And unexpectedly beautiful. Colonised by lichen, this is the old stuff, persuaded down to the sea by channels carved out of the side of the hill by humans desperate to divert molten lava away from villages. Nature's indifferent rampage nurtured into the soothing arms of the sea. Again, I'm impressed by the little Panda. It feels grown-up and capable, and, after pottering for a while, we finally arrive at the base of Etna feeling a little more robust about our chances, eventually pulling up at the place where the cable car starts and most civilian traffic stops. Today, though, we have The Permissions, and the barriers rise for us.

Somewhat inevitably, there's a dark green first-generation Panda 4x4 at the bottom of the mountain. It's the Sisley special edition, still wearing the Steyr-Puch badges. Fondness swells. It's tiny, with tyres barely a handspan wide, and so tinny and basic it could have come free with a box of Sicilian cereal. But there are lots of cues that point to our newer Panda, and it exudes the kind of straight-edged, fuss-free charm it's impossible to engineer with modern, crash-safe cars. A brief conversation with the owner, and it turns out this Panda has covered 380,000km (about 236,000 miles) on its original engine. Actually, no one really knows how far it's been, because for 'some years' in the nineties, the speedo was broken.

There are, of course, easier ways to get up Mount Etna than Panda-based transport. There's a cable car that can take you about two-thirds of the way – though you still have to hike the last bit to get to the very top – or off-road buses that can deliver you to a point at the base of the biggest caldera. The 'buses' are serious bits of off-road kit, based as they are on the Mercedes Unimog, and the Fiat seems comprehensively outgunned parked next to one, which, again, doesn't augur particularly cheerfully.

It's not too long before we realise why the Etna taxi service needs such hardcore rigs. The 'road' up the side of Etna is basically a track bulldozed along the line of least resistance. So it meanders like an old man's conversation: a series of switchbacks here and there, a long straight bit, a

LEFT (OPPOSITE PAGE): *Etna consists of steep roads, loose surfaces, much snow and no barriers. This calls for a spot of four-wheel-drive!*

LEFT (THIS PAGE): *'What, me? Just driving up an erupting volcano during an earthquake. Beats a day in the Top Gear office…'*

BELOW: *Some of the tracks up mount Etna end abruptly. Take care. Otherwise you'll drive into the crater and melt to death*

sometimes on snow, sometimes on that gently steaming black sand. A spooky situation. No other 4x4 could get here, because not even the most hardcore SUV could have inveigled itself into the position a humble little Fiat has managed, for the simple reason they would fall off the side and die. I'm not going to think about that for a little while.

The going is getting increasingly tough though, and the Panda requires higher revs to maintain forward momentum, the occasions we resort to the low first gear to claim supremacy over lumps getting ever more frequent. The hard-packed lava sand is easy enough to find purchase on, but as soon as we try to traverse the snowy bits – or the looser lava marbles with the steam rising between them – the Panda's skinny tyres start to cut into the surface rather than float over it. With only 75bhp and 107lb ft of torque to play with, and the thinning atmosphere adding an asthmatic intake of oxygen, eventually we hit a deep patch of snow, the Panda bogs and huffs to a stop. Only 100ft from the ridge line and a victory of sorts.

We try to dig the car further up, but every time the 4x4 engages to try to lift the car higher, the lack of grip and meaningful torque from low enough in the rev range means that the Panda is sucked to a dead stop. Well, that, and the clutch smoke pouring out of the bonnet after one particularly vigorous effort. After what seems like an age, we dig the Panda out of its resting place and happily canter off back down Mount Etna with blessed relief. There's a sense of pregnancy about Etna, of bloat and indigestion, and it's making the hairs on the back of my neck stand up. But after a bit, I decide that I'm imagining it, and we stop to take a final few pictures. I stare back up the steep, gravelly slopes and realise that the Panda 4x4, this little 15-grand hatchback, has taken us further than any of the big, expensive SUVs could have possibly hoped. Up a living volcano. It may be a small car, but it has a huge heart. Sometime later, we pad down the hill, send the Panda home and retire to the airport, convinced that the feeling of portent leaking from Etna was all in our imagination.

We were – of course – wrong. As we boarded our plane home, Mount Etna erupted, spewing a small trickle of molten lava down the side of the mountain a couple of hundred feet from where we were stuck. Which goes to prove two things: one, that Pandas always fare better out in the wild, and two, that the bit about avoiding smoking mountains remains terribly good advice.

THE QUIET REVOLUTION

TO THE WORLD'S MOST DANGEROUS BORDER IN A TINY GREEN CAR. WHO NEEDS A TANK, EH?

A boiled silkworm looks and probably tastes like a wet woodlouse. I choose one from a cup of steaming larvae and cautiously lick its ribbed body. It smells like the inside of a reptile house and, despite being dead, slips down my throat with a wriggle. For South Koreans it's a tasty snack, sold in the weirder corners of Seoul, which, right now, feels like some sort of night circus.

I buy mine from a clown. As he stirs his cauldron of grubs, we're passed by a horse-drawn carriage, shaped like a pumpkin and lit with neon. Over the road, there's a patio full of huge plastic mushrooms and a lifeless model of Snow White. And here comes a stormtrooper on a moped, with a flashing red heart on a stick. What the hell do they put in their silkworms?

Back to the car. Shut the door. Weaving through the backstreets of its home city, the little green Kia is a bubble of sanity among the strangeness – a fluorescent metaphor for South Korea's journey from the havoc of wartime to economic enormity. A prime example of how this place is spooking big businesses, not with cheap substitutes, but with properly desirable stuff, from smartphones to tellies to cars. Finally, here's a Korean supermini that you might choose over, say, a Fiat 500. You want a bargain? The car we have here is a touch over 10 grand, but you can have one for under eight.

Onwards through the mayhem, being careful not to squish a foot. The road is full of entangled young couples, full of rice wine. A man stands in front of us, slaps both hands on the bonnet and gurns

WHERE IS IT?
East Asia

WHICH BIT?
From Seoul to the DMZ near Cheorwon

GIVE ME CO-ORDINATES!
38.161116, 127.312680

WHEN SHOULD I GO?
Technically there's still a war going on between the North and South, so check the news first…

HOW LONG WILL IT TAKE?
You should manage the round-trip in a day

HOW DO I GET THERE?
Loads of airlines fly to Seoul. Then hire a car and follow Route 43 out of town

WHAT'S THE WEATHER LIKE?
Damp

WHAT'S THE ROAD LIKE?
Potholed

WHAT IF I GET LOST?
Watch your step – there are roadside landmines north of Cheorwon

TG TOP TIP:
To get this close to the DMZ you'll need to talk nicely to the authorities in Cheorwon

ONE MORE THING:
If you're lucky, they'll give you some paperwork and escort you through the checkpoints

widely, mirroring the lower half of the Picanto's steering wheel. His girlfriend peels him away and they disappear through a doorway into a karaoke bar, stacked right under an indoor baseball range. This place is one huge cultural mash-up, with some bits borrowed from America (tens of thousands of US troops are stationed here) and others from an Oriental acid trip. Frank Sinatra spills from one bar, squeaky K-pop from another. 'Yummy yummy yummy, now show me the money!' sings a man in a food shack.

Out of the rat runs, the oddness morphs into a more familiar cityscape. You might imagine a chaotic picture of tuk-tuks and manky dogs, but Seoul is much further up the food chain than that. The buildings are tall and glassy, the tarmac's fresh and the cars are homegrown – only a handful aren't Hyundais or Kias or SsangYongs. It's the same ratio for interesting paintjobs, and our Picanto – a right-hand-drive car destined for Britain – is a flash of brightness in a monochrome sea of saloons. Traffic moves fast, and if you're not nosing the car in front, you'll be carved up by a taxi. But there's no road rage, and few horn blasts. You just get the sense that everyone's in a hurry to get things done.

Across town, past the Seoul Museum of Chicken Arts and over the river. At a set of traffic lights – evidently synced to a tide clock – the Picanto draws long looks. Not long ago, Korean city cars had the visual elegance of a Zimmer frame. The Picanto is the first one to feel properly styled. All the big elements are pushed to the

CHEORWON

Yeongbuk-myeon

Pocheon

Uijeongbu

Dobong-gu

Gangbuk-gu

SEOUL

corners so it seems larger than it is, while the sharp waistline dissects the high sides so it looks sculpted not slabby. The headlights are very expensive-looking things with a complex layout of tubes and twinkly bulbs, which link the chunky front end to the rest of the car to create a sense of solidity. It feels confident in its own skin without relying on retro or pastiche.

As the night lifts like a stage curtain, we drift around the streets for a while. This is a city of 11 million people, and, going by the early-hours traffic, about half of them have impatient alarm clocks. So, with silkworms somewhat digested, we go in search of breakfast. With most shop signs written in Korean, and not wishing to inadvertently visit a brothel ('Funny story, darling…'), I follow a van with a picture of something foody. Must be delivering somewhere nearby.

We turn off the highway and loop around an interchange into a fish market. It's a long, low warehouse, stocked with a haul from the Yellow Sea. Security seems relaxed – or more accurately, asleep – so we drive in, tyres squelching past tanks of live octopus, tentacles flicking against the wing mirrors. There are alien crustaceans, silver angelfish, many unidentified squirmy things, and the sort of smell that could only come from buckets of old fish heads. That, and the fattest, happiest cat you've ever seen.

Appetites curiously suppressed, we emerge into a yellowy dawn. A quick swig from a can of Pocari Sweat – A Morning Eye Opener! – and we're on the expressway out of town. There's a thick smog over the city, ghosting skyscrapers against the hills. Heading east, the glassy architecture gives way to uniform high-rises. They're all painted the same shade of peach, or maybe it's faded pink,

FAR LEFT (OPPOSITE PAGE): *'Just popping out for a silkworm, love. If I'm not back by sunrise, send help. Or a pack of Rennie – the minty ones'.*

LEFT (THIS PAGE): *Believe it or not, this is a road. And the Korean girls are not an incentive to keep an eye on it.*

BELOW: *The Picanto leaves Seoul, heading for the North Korean border and a staring match with a short, fat dictator*

and each has a number: Samsung 101, Hyundai 102...
huge monoliths of the MegaCorps that turned Seoul from
fifties bombsite to modern metropolis. Back then, Kia
was still making tubes for bicycle frames.

The Picanto flies past. It feels more solid than its bargain
status would suggest. There's something very grown
up about the way it drives, from the smooth 1.25-litre
petrol to the damping that feels far more intelligent than
anything else at this price – softish front springs to absorb
whacks around town, stiffish rear beam to keep things
tidy through corners. And I'm not sure if a car has ever
done a stoppie, but the brakes bite hard enough to give it
a go. The interior is basic, but boosted by a wave of silver
across the dashboard. The dials have simple fonts and
white backlights, the seats are comfy and adults fit in the
back. The steering could be a bit crisper and the stereo
less tinny, but if those are the only downers in the deal,
we're happy.

With the buildings thinning out, we begin the climb
into the hills. About 70 per cent of the Korean Peninsula
is mountainous, and many countrysiders have moved to
big cities and those tower blocks. So the road is ours. We
streak past pig farms, rising higher, aiming north. We're
about 30 miles out of town now, the sun is up and the
road curls away into the distance. Foot down. Sniff farm
odour. Avoid Humvees. Down the hill they come, two
of them, big and green and wider than the road. We're
showered by grit and forced into the weeds.

This is military country. A worryingly short stone's
throw away from Seoul is the North Korean border,
one of the most heavily militarised places on Earth.
Technically, the borderline isn't militarised at all – it runs
through the centre of the demilitarised zone, a 2.5-mile
buffer between North and South – but on either side of
that divide, each country is armed to the eyeballs. Bill
Clinton once described it as 'the scariest place on Earth',
a no-man's-land between one world – our world – and
a much darker one. In another few miles, the regular
civilian road will end. There's a further buffer before
the DMZ, a military area that's off-limits to most cars.
Except ours. In the town of Cheorwon, we deploy our
silver-tongued *TopGear* agent to the local government
office and he returns with a bit of paper. It says we can
continue, right up to the DMZ fence.

We roll northwards across a river, where the road runs

through a huge concrete corridor as high as a house. It's a tank trap, designed to implode when the charges are blown, blocking the road or – with some particularly malicious timing – falling on top of whatever's passing through. Little green Kias included. Deep breath, first gear, all the revs, through the gauntlet and onwards to the 38th Parallel. Shortly afterwards, we're stopped again, this time at a checkpoint. The road is blocked by oil drums, arranged in the rather tempting shape of a chicane. A soldier inspects our paperwork and another stands guard, his rifle (standard issue Daewoo K2) pointed at our tyres. Deep breath, first gear, all the revs…

They salute us through. The road flattens, and we're on a plateau, speeding across rice fields on a raised causeway. Ahead is the DMZ, stretching 160 miles from one side of the country to the other. At the final checkpoint, we're ushered up to an observation area, closer to the fence line than any civilian car has been before. From here, we can clearly see the jaggedy Kim Il Sung Highlands in the North, and a whole section of the Zone, lined by razorwire and watchtowers, snaking away into the hills. It's the same in the North, as troops engage in a permanent staring match across the divide. Between them is one of the world's biggest landmine fields, untouched by humans since 1953, bar wanabee defectors from the North, some of which make it, most of which don't. It's so wild it's become a marshy nature reserve, home to Asiatic tigers, wild boar and rare bean geese, presumably all of which tread very carefully.

But despite the looming threat of sniper fire, it all feels very peaceful. Some red-crowned cranes warble overhead. Over the years, this border has been pushed and pulled in each direction, but, someday, when North Korea meets its fate, it may be dissolved completely. People split by war will be reunited. They will join forces to make even better tellies and smarter phones and more cars like the Picanto. The revolution will continue. Kia? It's only just getting started.

BURMA

DISTANCE: 973 MILES

CAR: THREE OLD LORRIES

TOP GEAR TELLY TRIP: TRUCKING IN BURMA

'Being the most experienced horseman, I took the frisky, five-legged stallion.'
Hammond

'Gone are the days when you simply turned up with a glovebox full of strong pornography and egg on your vest'
Clarkson

Pyin Oo Lwin

Keng Tung

Taunggyi

TACHILEIK

Naypyitaw

Tharrawaddy

YANGON (Rangoon)

your turn!

WHERE IS IT?
Myanmar, just to the west of Thailand

WHICH BIT?
From Yangon (Rangoon) to the Thai border, in a roundabout way

GIVE ME CO-ORDINATES!
18.923917, 96.332726

WHEN SHOULD I GO?
November to February

HOW LONG WILL IT TAKE?
Two weeks, if you plan right

HOW DO I GET THERE?
Most flights to Yangon connect in Bangkok

WHAT'S THE WEATHER LIKE?
Clammy

WHAT'S THE ROAD LIKE?
Rutted

WHAT IF I GET LOST?
In some areas there's no phone signal, so arm yourself with maps and a decent GPS

TG TOP TIP:
Rental cars are rare, so consider buying something cheap or going alfresco on a motorbike

ONE MORE THING:
There are still pockets of conflict in the Shan State, so be careful where you venture and don't be daft

BEHIND THE WALL

WITH THE GENGHIS KHAN TOURIST GUIDE TO CHINA IN HAND, TG EMBARKS ON A ROAD TRIP IN SEARCH OF THE GREAT WALL. HOW HARD CAN IT BE?

The sole English sentence on my last can of energy drink does not make reassuring reading. No list of ingredients. Distilled pig adrenaline and black magic, judging by its effect on my heart rate and general paranoia. Whatever's in it is only contributing to the unnerving sensation that *TopGear* has just wandered into a Chinese version of *The Shining*.

It is past midnight on a tundra-cold night in Inner Mongolia, and we have arrived, in our copper-red RCZ, at the weirdest hotel this side of Kubrick's Overlook. Silhouetted over a tiny village, an ominous, out-of-scale monstrosity, an imperious sprawl of grand building, wings, courtyards and towers, a thousand-room behemoth. Completely empty. Deserted. We park up in a courtyard with space for 500 cars. The RCZ is alone.

Reception is icy. A tiny creature emerges from a back room and silently hands us our keys. She knows who we are. Her only guests. Traipsing the long, long corridor to my room, it is a surprise not to encounter a small child on a tricycle or a pair of evil, blue-dressed twins.

The plan was a straightforward one: to take the RCZ to find the Great Wall of China. Not the prissy, touristy bit right outside Beijing, but the real, unrestored, Mongol-repelling thing. A nerve-mincing night's drive, weaving between dawdling, dark lorries on inky mountain roads, has led us to Asia's creepiest hotel. I lie awake and listen to pipes creak and scream – please, God, let them be pipes –

WHERE IS IT?
The People's Republic of China

WHICH BIT?
From Beijing to Xi Shui Yu Cun

GIVE ME CO-ORDINATES!
40.408067, 116.313621

WHEN SHOULD I GO?
Autumn is the Goldilocks season: not too warm, not too chilly, not too wet and not too dry

HOW LONG WILL IT TAKE?
Depends how quickly you find the Wall...

HOW DO I GET THERE?
Pick any road north from Beijing, but keep an eye on traffic – one jam lasted for ten whole days

WHAT'S THE WEATHER LIKE?
Oriental

WHAT'S THE ROAD LIKE?
Brittle

WHAT IF I GET LOST?
Find a section of Wall and walk along it. Eventually it'll lead you to civilisation

TG TOP TIP:
There are plenty of touristy places to see the Wall, but for a less gimmicky experience, follow our route

ONE MORE THING:
Chinese driving standards can be erratic. Stay alert and watch out for oncoming tuktuks

and console myself with the thought that, tomorrow, we will wake in the very shadow of mankind's greatest feat of engineering.

The next morning, we emerge into the half-light of frozen late autumn. The Great Wall is not here. Nowhere to be seen. *TopGear* is prolific at losing important things – car keys, insurance documents, occasionally photographers – but mislaying the world's largest man-made structure is a new low. A short but heated conversation, and blame is laid at my 1:8,000,000 scale tourist map, which apparently isn't detailed enough to navigate accurately across deepest China.

We have lost the Great Wall, but have found the 1950s. Maybe the 1850s. This is rural China, a million miles from Beijing and its high-rise developments and gridlock. Ancient women, ossified by the cold and dry, push wrought-iron bicycles along the dusty streets, baskets loaded high with corn and unidentified bits of metal. In this copper-red shade, against a backdrop of tiny blacksmith stalls and dusty kiosks, the RCZ looks better than ever, sculpted arches and sleek rear deck. It's a grower, this car. Don't think this excuses your eyesores of the last decade, Peugeot, but the RCZ is starting to look like a design icon.

An ancient toothy man with a child's face – his face, I mean, not an actual... oh, forget it – wanders over and gives the RCZ a big thumbs-up. We open the driver's door to show him around, and he nods approvingly.

'Chinese?' he asks hopefully.

XI SHUI YU CUN

Changlingzhen

Changping

Shahezhen

Huilongguanzhen

Chaoyang

BEIJING

ABOVE: *Our RCZ makes an escape from Beijing, heading north to the countryside. It was blue before it met China's mucky roads.*

LEFT: *This is the inside of a car. If you get stuck in a Chinese traffic jam, it'll be your home for a week.*

FAR RIGHT (OPPOSITE PAGE): *Tuk Tuks, feral chickens and bright red Peugeot coupes. Just your typical medieval street scene in rural Asia.*

'No, French,' I reply apologetically.

'Chinese?' he tries again, smiling a big smile.

'Definitely French. Peugeot,' I point at the badge. 'French.'

Our friend considers for a moment, brow wrinkled. 'Chinese!' he cheers, and trips off down the street, delighted to have won the argument. Case settled: the RCZ is Chinese. Who knew?

We depart the village on a chalky single-track road and join a highway that, a petrol-station attendant assures us as we fill up with fuel that smells of cheap scrumpy, will spirit us straight to the Great Wall. On the opposite side of the carriageway, a monster traffic jam snakes into the distance. On and on it stretches: 20, 25, 30 miles of gridlocked lorries. No cars, no buses, just thousands of trucks, carrying livestock, rocks, rubbish. The truckers – who have been trapped all night, maybe longer – look haunted, broken. It could be worse, guys. Two months before we headed to China,

a road near here was awarded the dubious distinction of hosting the world's longest traffic jam: 70 miles and 10 days of total standstill.

On our side of the road, though, the traffic is light; dotted across the carriageways are a few dawdling lorries, between which the RCZ spears with ease. This top-spec 200bhp version, with its 1.6-litre turbo lump, is a quick little car, with more punch than its 7.5-second 0–60mph time suggests. In the hands of a good driver on a twisty road it'll happily keep tabs on more exotic machinery, and it devours smooth motorways with a fluency and ease that most small hot cars simply can't manage.

We turn off the carriageway – praying fervently we don't confuse our exits and end up at the back of the Trucker Log-jam – and swing towards the mountains. A few miles along this empty, desolate track, we pass the rusting ruins of a petrol station.

Actually, calling it a petrol station is like calling the HMS Ark Royal a dinghy. A 60m^2 pyramid hoisted 20m

off the ground decays slowly under the harsh sun, its pumps piled up in one corner, its restaurants and rows of shops derelict and abandoned. The two-lane road alongside it used to form the main route between Beijing and the north. When a new highway was built to the east, the services became obsolete. Not an unusual story in itself, but the strange bit is that no one has bothered to reuse any part of the structure. Don't bother tearing it down and recycling the materials, just build a new one down the road. It's a hulking metaphor for the Chinese attitude to raw materials.

In a tiny, bustling market town, we park up under the central drum tower to stock up on water and unidentifiable snack products. About us, barrows are stacked feet-high with chillis the size of children's forearms. The three-tier tower forms the road's central reservation, cars, rickshaws, bicycles and three-wheelers orbiting in both directions, weaving in and out of each other's path at pace, all the while avoiding a pile-up. There is a rehearsed serenity to the proceedings, like every actor has performed this same scene a million times before. We ask a few locals the way to the Wall. They all point vaguely towards the highest mountain peaks. Big stony thing, top of the hills. Can't miss it.

Oh, we can. It isn't quite as ridiculous as it sounds to lose the Great Wall. But the medieval wonder isn't really a single wall, rather a whole series of fortifications scattered over northern China and built over 2,000 years, so finding it isn't the simple task of driving north until you bump into it. Add in the fact that most of the Wall clings to the top of precipitous mountains, far from the valley-hugging roads, and it turns out that an eight-metre high, four-thousand-mile structure is actually a slippery little bugger to find.

Late afternoon. We haven't found the Wall. As compensation, however, we have discovered a perfect facsimile of the perfect Alpine pass. China's liberal attitude to intellectual property is the source of much angst in Europe, but this is one carbon copy they're welcome to: two freshly surfaced lanes zig-zagging through cool trees, climbing higher and higher into the terracotta mountains. The RCZ comes alive. It is a beautifully balanced car, this, easy to drive quickly. It isn't perfect – the most significant niggle is the spiky clutch, which does all its work in the first few

AFRICA

DISTANCE: 880 MILES

CAR: BMW 528i, SUBARU IMPREZA
WRX, BMW 850R

TOP GEAR TELLY TRIP: FINDING THE SOURCE OF THE NILE

'It's probably safe to say the
Victorian explorers didn't
face problems are as big as
this. Now this is what you
call a traffic jam'
– Clarkson

'That's all completely hopeless,
you've sunk the raft, and your
cat flap's terrible.'
– May

Map labels: Fort Portal, Mubende, Kampala, JINJA, Kasese, UGANDA, Bushenyi, Ntungamo, Lake Victoria, Nyagatare, RWANDA, GRUMET RIVER, Kibungo, Mwanza, Nyabugombe, Kasama, Buseresere, BURUNDI, TANZANIA

WHERE IS IT?
Africa. Big place. Can't miss it

WHICH BIT?
From Uganda to Tanzania

GIVE ME CO-ORDINATES!
-2.557514, 30.884413

WHEN SHOULD I GO?
July and August are the least clammy

HOW LONG WILL IT TAKE?
How long do you have?

HOW DO I GET THERE?
A well-known British airline goes non-stop to Entebbe Airport from Europe

WHAT'S THE WEATHER LIKE?
Hot and heavy

WHAT'S THE ROAD LIKE?
Boggy

WHAT IF I GET LOST?
Watch out for poachers

TG TOP TIP:
Book a night in the Mewya Safari Lodge on Lake Edward. The view is excellent, and so is the wildlife

ONE MORE THING:
Did you know that hippos run faster than humans? Sleep well now!

FARE GAME

WHAT'S IT LIKE TO BE A CABBIE IN A CITY WHERE THE STREETS HAVE NO NAME? WE MEET A MASTER OF THE NIGHT

There are many surprising things about a Tokyo taxi, but the first to strike me is the rear door. I bend forward to pull the handle but it's too late, the driver's pressed the auto release button and set several kilos of glass and metal on an unstoppable arc towards my head. As I weep, a blurry figure hurries over. 'Daniel-san! So sorry! Here, take energy drink. Good for health!' My accidental assailant is Yukio Sudow, a 68-year-old Tokyoite and our guide to this mysterious metropolis. We met yesterday when his yellow cab appeared at the perfect moment to save me from a street hawker. Tonight he's agreed to show us the secret world of the nocturnal cabbie in a place where most streets are nameless and the roadmap looks like an unraveled ball of string.

At less than five feet tall, Sudow-san is dwarfed by his car. His suit hangs loosely around his tiny frame, his trousers smother little purple shoes, and his cuffs overlap white gloves more suited to a snooker referee. He loads our gear into the boot, then bows briefly before ushering me through the door – now safely open – and onto a rear seat upholstered almost entirely with doilies. There's a clear sneeze guard between driver and rear passenger, neatly displayed certificates and identification, a console festooned with a credit card reader and fare meter and radio, plus a wicker basket full of sweets on the dashboard. This is a Toyota Crown Comfort, the most common cab in town. Despite looking like something from the eighties, it's actually just 10 years old, a sort of modern-vintage oddity like the Nissan Cedric, the second most common cab, both of which are still made and sold as commercial vehicles in Japan.

WHERE IS IT?
Japan, obviously

WHICH BIT?
From Shibuya Crossing to the Skytree

GIVE ME CO-ORDINATES!
35.681636, 139.729829

WHEN SHOULD I GO?
Whenever, but make the most of the jetlag and go for a nocturnal drive

HOW LONG WILL IT TAKE?
About 25 minutes point-to-point, but stop and see some stuff

HOW DO I GET THERE?
You have the internet. On it, you can book a return flight to Tokyo for about £800 to £1,000

WHAT'S THE WEATHER LIKE?
Honourable

WHAT'S THE ROAD LIKE?
Unfathomable

WHAT IF I GET LOST?
The streets often have no names, so this is highly likely. Satnav is your savior

TG TOP TIP:
For once, let someone else do the driving. Hail a cab and enjoy the sightseeing

ONE MORE THING:
Public transport stops around midnight, when demand for taxis spikes. Wait until the rush dies down

---

It's about 11 o'clock, approaching the golden hour of the taxi when the trains stop running and people are too dizzy to walk, let alone take control of a car. Almost everything on wheels is a cab. They line curbs for whole blocks, long caterpillars of yellow and green and blue. Entire intersections are clotted with Crowns and Cedrics as they creep through the unfathomable network of ground-level streets. We begin at Shibuya Crossing, Tokyo's version of Piccadilly Circus, only twice as big and twice as bright. Except recently about half the bulbs have been dulled to save energy after the Fukushima energy crisis. But still, great pillars of light shine down on the street as the last office workers emerge from their boxrooms in search of sake or a ride home.

Sudow-san has been ferrying them around for 18 years. He was once a bricklayer, but quit when the economy boomed and there was more cash to be made in cabbing. He passed his map exam first time and has since taken around a hundred thousand fares. But his window on the world hasn't turned him into some prowling, mohawked De Niro. Instead, he's risen through the taxi ranks to become a Mr Miyagi, a grand master recognised by an official 'A' rating, and tutor to young students of the trade. He teaches road manners inspired by Buddhism, and appears to have invented some sort of Zen roadcraft. He sits comfortably with his legs apart, resting one hand on his knee, the other on the wheel. A booster seat helps him see over the dashboard. The essence of good taxi driving, he says, is to be patient,

SKYTREE

Changlingzhen

Takebashi

Nagatacho

Shinanomachi

Sangubashi

SHIBUYA CROSSING

friendly and industrious. He'll never join those long queues outside train stations, preferring to cruise the streets while mentally signposting their chaotic addresses. Blocks and buildings have digits not names, numbered in the order they were built regardless of how they're placed. But no matter how obscure your destination or how much kebab is on your face, he'll always go south of the river.

We peel off a long, neon avenue and up a ramp to the expressway, one of many that soar through the city, raised up like vast aqueducts, pouring traffic between buildings before draining back down through looping intersections. A tollbooth barrier raises at the last moment as we blast through at 50mph, playing a high-speed game of chicken with potentially decapitous consequences. The elevated roads are fast and curvy and the perfect place for some illegal street racing. Sudow-san takes it easy, but back in the nineties this is where the original Midnight Club brought their tuned Skylines and NSXs and Supras, with new members required to reach at least 150mph for initiation (at which point someone might nudge their rear bumper, just so they could taste the fear). After a police crackdown, it's less common to see them now, though we are passed by a fast-moving

GT-R, a streak of purple against the grey concrete.

From up here, the lower streets look like sluggish rivers of light, occasionally frozen for an earthquake drill when a siren sounds and cars must stop on the spot, scattered like power-starved dodgems. We exit the expressway down a slope where the road is swallowed by a tunnel into the sodium-soaked Tokyo underworld, a labyrinth of subways bored into the Earth alongside hundreds of train tunnels and walkways. We surface a minute later into the slightly less murky Kabukichō red-light district. Traffic slows, the streets tighten and through the window comes the romantic sound of Lionel Richie, piped from love hotels that rent dark rooms to newly acquainted couples by the hour. Sudow-san doesn't venture here often, due mostly to a law that stops him picking up drunks who might redecorate the neat and tidy cabin.

A few blocks away we pick up our first and only fare (apparently people are a little wary of sharing the rear bench with an unexplained Englishman). Takuya Imura treats himself to a taxi once a week, rather than suffer on the packed metro system where men are employed solely to shove people into carriages. He used to hail one more often. When smoking was banned in bars and on pavements, but still legal in taxis, he'd leave his drink and

ABOVE: *A cab at Shibuya Crossing – a concrete sandwich of roads, walkways, train tracks and expressways. Get it wrong here and you'll be lost for years.*

LEFT: *Yukio Sudow: grand master cabbie and pioneering navigator, capable of most honorable speeds through narrow tollbooths.*

FAR LEFT (OPPOSITE PAGE): *Unless you have a freakish knowledge of Tokyo's street numbers, you're better off in one of these.*

request a lap of the block for a crafty but rather expensive smoke – there's a standard five-quid fee before you've moved an inch. Turns out Takuya is one of Sudow-san's less eventful customers. Over the years, Japanese comedians, actors, and even sumo wrestlers have sat back here. Someone once left some false teeth behind. Thankfully the gummy owner also left a mobile phone and was fully re-dentured within an hour. Other drivers have been less fortunate, and in a recent book, *Taxis: The Real Story*, one Tokyo cabbie claims he was used as an unwitting getaway driver for a Yakuza heist. On another occasion, someone left him a full bag of dead cats.

We drop Takuya outside his apartment and he pays up. Sudow-san pulls out a wallet of cash, none of which could be described as local tender. He shows me notes bearing faces of queens and rulers from Singapore to the States, souvenirs of his travels that he likes to carry around with him. 'Daniel-san, look,' he says. 'This one – Jamaica. Yeah, man!' He giggles like someone's tickled his feet. He tells me he likes to explore the world, a useful trait when you're a cabbie in a city measuring 60 miles across. He also likes to fish, and on days off he takes a little motorboat out in Tokyo Bay to spend a few hours waiting for a horse mackerel to take the bait. Tomorrow is a day off, and the one after, and the one after that. Like lots of Tokyo cabbies he works just eight days per month, cramming them with a month's worth of work. An average shift lasts 20 hours or more.

Which is why you'll often find cabs parked in backstreets with rear doors open and a little pair of feet dangling out. There's a law that says each shift must be punctuated with at least one snack and sleep break, though it doesn't stipulate for how long. So drivers park for a power snooze before downing an energy drink and driving through the night. Sudow-san likes to take his under the Tokyo Tower, a communications beacon in the middle of the city painted white and 'international orange' to alert wayward pilots of its presence. On first impression it might not look it, but it's actually nine metres taller than its Paris counterpart, possessing a deceptive majesty just like the man sleeping beneath it. And it's here that we leave him, to his dreams of faraway places and strange fish. If you're ever in town, have a go at finding him. He'll be your bubble of calm in this weird world. Wait beside the road – for days if you have to – and if you see him coming, jump out. Plant both hands on the bonnet. Ask to go anywhere. Just mind your head on the way in.

INDIA

DISTANCE: 1,325 MILES

CAR: JAGUAR XJS, ROLLS ROYCE
SILVER SHADOW, MINI COOPER

TOP GEAR TELLY TRIP: ACROSS INDIA

'In the morning, the dual carriageway madness continued. Only now, we could actually see what was going to kill us'
– Hammond

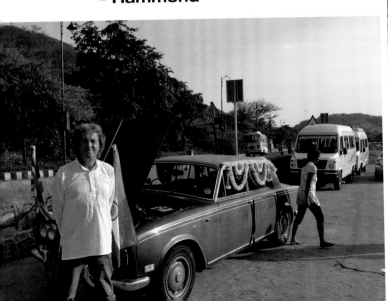

My pillow was just a pillowcase... my sleeping bag broke, my blanket was see-through, my body was down to a temperature hitherto unknown to science.
– Clarkson

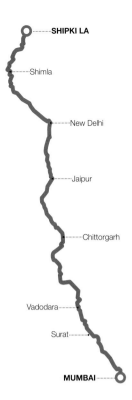

SHIPKI LA

Shimla

New Delhi

Jaipur

Chittorgarh

Vadodara

Surat

MUMBAI

your turn!

WHERE IS IT?
Asia. Right in the middle

WHICH BIT?
From Mumbai to Shipki La

GIVE ME CO-ORDINATES!
29.066273, 77.062416

WHEN SHOULD I GO?
Monsoons last from July to September.
So not then

HOW LONG WILL IT TAKE?
Precisely 32 hours

HOW DO I GET THERE?
A flight to Mumbai should do the trick

WHAT'S THE WEATHER LIKE?
Muggy

WHAT'S THE ROAD LIKE?
Farmy

WHAT IF I GET LOST?
Mind the cows

TG TOP TIP:
From Mumbai, take the Superfast
Express Train to Jaipur. It's an
overnighter with room for your car

ONE MORE THING:
This route takes you to the Tibetan border
in the Himalayas, but you could stop in Delhi

BUGGY HELL

TWO SORE MEN, NO SHOWERS, AND A THOUSAND MILES OF MEXICAN MADNESS

We're in a strip joint in Tijuana. This wasn't part of the plan. One moment, I was flaked out in the back of a van fresh off a long-haul flight; the next, I have a Corona in my hand, an equally shell-shocked photographer at my side, and close-quarters writhing is happening, lit red and bouncing to a deep beat. A man with a cruel face squares up to me. 'What ju here for? You want woman? We've got l-o-t-s of womaaan.' He drags the syllables out.

'Um. No thank you, not at the moment.'

'Ju here for the Ba-ha, right? I got gurrrls from aaall over Meh-hee-co. Everyone here for the Ba-ha. Gurrrls here for Ba-ha.'

The Baja 1000 is legendary. Not because – ahem – related service industries expand to meet demand while the race is on, but because this is the world's longest and most gruelling non-stop off-road race, a southbound blast down the finger of land that marks much of Mexico's Pacific coast. It's the biggest sporting event in the country, with an estimated 1.5 million spectators lining the 1,121.55-mile (sometimes it's a few more or less) route. And it's not even held on a weekend. Perhaps a national holiday has been declared.

Justin the photographer and I are here to take part. For me, this is something I've wanted to do forever, real bucket-list stuff. Justin's only bucket-related thought is that we're going to kick it. It probably doesn't help that you're free to be fantastically underprepared; you need no special licence to do this, just a green wristband gained at signing on and a suitably gnarly car. Ours is a Baja Challenge buggy, and it looks smaller, lighter and faster than it actually is. It's powered by a naturally aspirated, rear-

WHERE IS IT?
On the Baja Peninsula

WHICH BIT?
From Ensenada to La Paz

GIVE ME CO-ORDINATES!
29.515120, -114.290332

WHEN SHOULD I GO?
Get there by mid November, or else you'll miss the start of the race

HOW LONG WILL IT TAKE?
Around 40 hours straight, if you're driving properly

HOW DO I GET THERE?
Fly to San Diego, rent a car and cross the border at Tijuana. Prepare for sniffer dogs

WHAT'S THE WEATHER LIKE?
Dusty

WHAT'S THE ROAD LIKE?
Road? You'll be lucky...

WHAT IF I GET LOST?
It's not if, but when. Take a proper co-driver and a military-grade GPS

TG TOP TIP:
Need wheels? Call the guys at Wide Open Tours – they'll sort you out with a suitably silly machine

ONE MORE THING:
You don't actually have to do the race. Less brutal trips are available all year round

---

mounted Subaru flat-four which sends 175bhp through a four-speed manual to the rear wheels. That's where the fun starts: 18in of suspension travel and a set of tyres more craggy than my driving coach's face.

Rich Minga is a Hollywood stuntman by day, but his dusty eyes, grizzled features and laidback demeanour are pure Baja. We're in the scrubby hills above the race-start town of Ensenada to get a feel for the car. For me, this is about driving, but Justin, with an expression not unlike the one he wore the previous evening, has just found out that, as co-driver, he's responsible for all navigation and communication. This includes 16 radio channels. Oh God.

'And you, my friend,' Rich says, turning to me, 'Well, this terrain ain't gonna teach you shit about the Baja.' Oh. I look out across the heavily eroded landscape, thankful at least that the race itself won't be as technically demanding as this mangled obstacle course of rock and earth. 'Nope,' Rich continues, kicking at the dirt. 'The Baja is a kick in the crotch compared with this soft-arse stuff.'

I do at least learn how to drive the 'car'. I learn that momentum is the single most important thing, that the gearbox is crummy, that there's no windscreen because it would be smashed by rocks, that the absence of doors aids egress when it rolls over, that I need to beware of the whoop-de-dos and that dust is an almighty issue. And I learn that I'll actually be glad that the steering has no feedback, no weight, yet is bewilderingly sharp. I have my doubts.

Aside from that, the buggy is a joyous device, something to be chucked at the landscape with wild abandon. Rich has witnessed my enthusiasm and decides a peg needs

ENSENADA

San Felipe

Coco's Corner

Bahia de Los Angeles

San Ignacio

San Juanico

Loreto

LA PAZ

to be removed from my confidence. 'You do realise how dangerous this event is?' I nod. 'That drunk spectators dick around with the course and build booby traps?' Slower nod. 'That faster cars will first tap, then ram you if you don't get out the way quick enough?' Small head movement. 'That people die out there every year?'

Race day: it's five hours to the start. Wanting Justin to have confidence in his driver, I tell him I've slept brilliantly. This is a lie. I keep quiet and start the complex procedure of getting dressed. There are many layers and lots of leads that have to be plugged in. Only one of these attaches to my penis. Others control airflow to the helmet, radio communications and drinking water. There's a kidney protector, a neck collar, a dust skirt and an anti-chafe vest. When we march down to the car, we do so in slo-mo, feeling like Apollo astronauts. BC-6 looks immaculate. We stow our gear and wave our team-mates off. You don't do the Baja solo – well, you can, but only if you're certifiable. The plan is that we'll do the first 400 miles before handing on to another pair, Jessi and Josh, who in turn will link up with a final pair, Steve and Doc (actually a dentist), for the last stint into

La Paz. Provided I give BC-6 to them in one piece. This is preying on my mind. We're the last of six cars in the Baja Challenge class. One and two are Baja veterans, aiming for good results. Cars three through five are being driven by a posse of Monster-sponsored extreme sports athletes. Much fist-bumping occurs from people whose crotches have less ground clearance than the cars they're driving. I look across at Justin and feel pity. I've done some rallying, but he's a motorsport virgin, and I've a nasty feeling I'm about to deflower him in the most brutal way possible.

The flag drops, I fail to fluff the start and we're away. Two corners on tarmac, then a hard right to Armageddon. We plunge down into a culvert. Third gear, keep it pinned, keep the nose high through the dirt and ruts. This is insane. People are everywhere, a funnel that parts as you charge towards them. It's Group B all over again. Big purpose-built jump. I'd promised myself I wouldn't lift for this, but the thing's eight foot high. Oh well, in for a penny…

Justin's whoop through the intercom is one of relief as we touch down smoothly and

TOP: *At the start of the race, our men had straight spines. By the end, they looked like antique accordions...*

FAR LEFT (OPPOSITE PAGE): *Our buggy, otherwise known as BC-6, heads down to the start line. Ollie and Justin cower just out of shot.*

LEFT: *It's less of cabin and more of a mudbath in here. This is good for healthy skin, but less good for camera kit.*

power on. Big puddle, colour of caramel. We have no mudguards, no windscreen. A wall of mucky water cascades in. Justin's camera sits unprotected on his lap. At mile 0.5 of 395, the Nikon's trashed. Some swearing. Rather belatedly, he shoves it into a waterproof bag. It doesn't dry out for 55 miles.

We're climbing up into the hills now, through rough quarries, rough slums, stray dogs, chanting crowds. Some try to point us the wrong way, others gesture correctly, but you never know who's who, and Justin's semaphore waving is proving decidedly erratic. BANG. Love-tap number one. Didn't even see him coming, what with the dust and all. I leap for the verge with flea-like speed, and let the bouncy Beetle by. By way of thanks, it sprinkles us with coarse grey gravel. This combines with the rain that started falling a few minutes earlier. I wipe my visor, wondering how long it will be before doing so will only make matters worse.

About 20 minutes is the answer. We rattle and bang down a steep gully into a silt bed. It's not a big one, maybe 200 metres across, but in between I can see three stuck trucks, two fountaining silt dust into the air, the other motionless bar some frantic shovelling. Momentum is everything. Low gear. Nail it. It's like driving into a rich brown snowdrift, as fine dust explodes up and hangs there, motionless. We seem to be paddling, not touching the bottom and lost in a dry brown pea-souper. I have an idea where we came in, and by some miracle we pop out in the right place, only at 90 degrees to my intended direction of travel. I don't lift, just turn sharp right, nerf a bank, scatter spectators and make my escape.

I glance at my co-driver. He looks like a freshly dug potato. All I can see is dry brown earth. It's coated everything. We can't read any of the switches; the screens are covered. We flap at them with gloved hands, but, already moist from the rain, everything now turns muddy. It continues in this vein until late afternoon, when we finally drop down out of the hills, clatter through a rock garden that would have been absurdly daunting three hours before and onto a road section. The relief is palpable. We've done 88 miles, in which we've banged tyres with a Class One buggy, cannoned through a blind yumps section, discovered our horn is actually a siren (fulfilling several childhood fantasies), very satisfyingly outbraked a 400bhp truck into a fast

pits are the most welcoming we've ever seen. Justin and I unbuckle harnesses and collapse into a brotherly hug. Twelve hours done. I pat the buggy. We're still last, an hour down, as Josh and Jessi head into the dark. It's the last we see of the buggy for 31 hours. They have a nightmare. Josh rolls, gets it stuck in silt, hits a motorbike, breaking the rider's foot, and having given himself the mental and physical jitters, hands driving duties back to Jessi. A wrong direction call sees them drive off a small cliff, breaking the front suspension, leading to a five-hour delay.

It limps home in 43 hours and 54 minutes, less than six minutes inside the 44-hour limit. But it's made it (one of fewer than 180 to do so, from a 300-strong starting list), even though Doc and Steve had to stop every 35 miles to buy power steering fluid from spectators. BC-6 dribbles on the podium. We smile, and toast with warm beer.

The Baja 1000 is a race that strips you, teaches you about pain thresholds, concentration levels, how you perform in adversity. It's the only racing I've ever done where the limiting factor isn't the car or the surface, but you. That's a tough lesson to learn. But we've done it, we made it. We fought the Baja, and we won.

FAR LEFT (OPPOSITE PAGE): *This is the Tizi N'tichka pass, which is even trickier to navigate that it is to pronounce. Unless you're Moroccan.*

LEFT (THIS PAGE): *Here's a fact: Victoria Beckham helped to design the Evoque. Maybe she did the floor mats or something.*

BELOW: *The Evoque meets a local donkey. Both are exceptionally good off-road, although the emissions are very different.*

DONKEYS, DEATH ROADS AND A DUSTER

CAN A CHEAP 4X4 SURVIVE THE SOUTHERN HEMISPHERE'S HARSHEST HILLS? THERE'S ONLY ONE WAY TO FIND OUT

Three vultures track the Duster up the dry, rocky canyon, gliding in silent formation 100 yards above the car as it bumps its way along the valley floor. They have decided, I think, that its occupants represent their best chance of lunch in this lifeless desert, a pair of gringos in a budget Romanian runabout on one of the world's wildest roads. The slaphead scavengers may have a point. We are winding up the notorious Cañón del Pato, a dirt track strung between Peru's arid coast and its dizzying Andean highlands, and I am wondering if *TopGear* has bitten off more than the little Dacia Duster can gummily chew. The Cañón del Pato – translates as 'Duck Canyon', contains

no ducks – should be approached with trepidation in a Toyota Land Cruiser or a military Humvee. But a £10,000 Eastern European SUV, a car that's too cheap to be badged a Renault? Gentlemen, prepare for your starring roles in *Carrion up the Canyon*!

I start to mentally compile a list of 'Things in Our Favour'. After 15 minutes it stands at this: (1) Four-wheel drive.

That's all I've got. A front-drive-only Duster is available but – ever safety-conscious – we've got the AWD version. That said, it's the sort of AWD system that, on paper at least, looks more suited to 'muddy driveway' than 'Peruvian death road'.

your turn!

WHERE IS IT?
High up in the Peruvian Andes

WHICH BIT?
From Chimbote to Huaraz, via the Cañón del Pato

GIVE ME CO-ORDINATES!
-8.743178, -77.913410

WHEN SHOULD I GO?
In the dry season, from January to March

HOW LONG WILL IT TAKE?
Roughly five hours each way

HOW DO I GET THERE?
It's a 260-mile drive from Lima to Chimbote, up the Pan-American Highway

WHAT'S THE WEATHER LIKE?
Vomitous

WHAT'S THE ROAD LIKE?
Plummety

WHAT IF I GET LOST?
Find a goat herder and deploy your finest Spanish. He shall guide you

TG TOP TIP:
Quit smoking. At this height the air is terrifyingly thin and you will probably be sick

ONE MORE THING:
Pato is Spanish for duck. Though you're more likely to see a guinea pig… on a dinner plate.

It remains front-drive in normal road use, a central clutch transferring up to 50 per cent of the power to the rear when it detects slippage. And that's about it for off-tarmac protection: the Duster is on road tyres, has no locking differentials, no winch and no water or food on board. Admittedly, the latter isn't really the Duster's issue so much as a total lack of forethought on the part of myself and photographer Matthias, but still the point stands: things ain't looking promising.

We are very much alone on this road. The last vehicle we saw was a rickety old bus bumbling the other way a few hours back, packed to the rafters with wan passengers and with the slogan 'JESUS ALONSO' across the top of the windscreen. Judging by the speed it passed at, the driver could indeed have been a hybrid of F1 ace and deity. Since then, nothing. Just miles and miles of brown-grey rock and corrugated track, snaking into the gargantuan Andes.

The odds are stacked against it, but the Duster is holding up. We clatter over rickety iron bridges laid with splintered planks of wood; we do motorway speeds across vicious terrain – hard rutted dirt cut with foot-deep holes and jagged, tyre-pinching boulders. The little Dacia (rhymes with 'Comin' Atcha', innit) shrugs it off with ease.

Past Yuracmarca, where an ancient man waves a live chicken at us like a magic wand, the canyon walls begin to close in, pinching atop the road like mile-high stage curtains. If ominous geology exists, this is it. Onwards and upwards, little Duster.

CHIMBOTE

Santo Toribio

Caraz

Yungay

Mancos

Carhuaz

HUARAZ

★★★★★

The Andes are big. If you are in possession of an atlas or a basic knowledge of geography, you may already be aware of this fact. But really, they're enormous – the biggest mountains in the world outside the Himalayas. Peru boasts some three dozen peaks over 19,000 feet, which, for the non-mountaineers among you, translates as 'really, really high'. But it's not just the size of the Andes, it's that they loom from nowhere: drive a few miles inland from Peru's arid, desert coast spring, and suddenly you're amidst monstrous, snow-capped giants, sheer sides rising almost vertically from valley floors. This place makes the Alps look like the Norfolk Broads.

Monstrous mountains mean colon-puckering mountain roads. Beyond the hydroelectric plant at Huallanca, the canyon track climbs violently, switchbacking up a steep face before diving into a tunnel

and emerging into the most freakish vista I have ever seen: a pair of opposing cliffs, each a couple of miles high, separated by barely 20 yards in places. The road is simply hacked along one straight-up cliff wall, a teetering path with 55 narrow tunnels blasted through the rock. There are no barriers, and the drop to the Río Santa below is – what? – 1,000 feet straight down. I locate my right testicle somewhere near my ribcage. This isn't misplaced fear: Peru boasts one of the worst vehicle death rates in the world, and this is one of its most dangerous roads. The Cañón del Pato is lined with makeshift crosses marking where cars, buses and trucks have plunged over the edge. The tunnels don't offer much respite. Barely a car's width in sections, they twist within the mountain, meaning you can't see what's coming the other way when you enter. There's only one thing for it: pray. And gun it.

My prayers and gunning don't work. In one of the longest tunnels, perhaps half a mile in, I spot the lights

FAR LEFT (OPPOSITE PAGE): *A tale of two donkeys: somewhere in remotest Peru, a traditional off-road load-lugger takes on modern equivalent. Loses wheezily.*

LEFT (THIS PAGE): *Six inches past Dacia's wing mirror lurks 2km vertical drop. This is Sam's Face Of Fear, which is similar to the Guinea Pig's.*

BELOW: *'Against Corruption', reads the slogan on this roadside graffiti. 'Unless it's really, really sneaky', says the next board…*

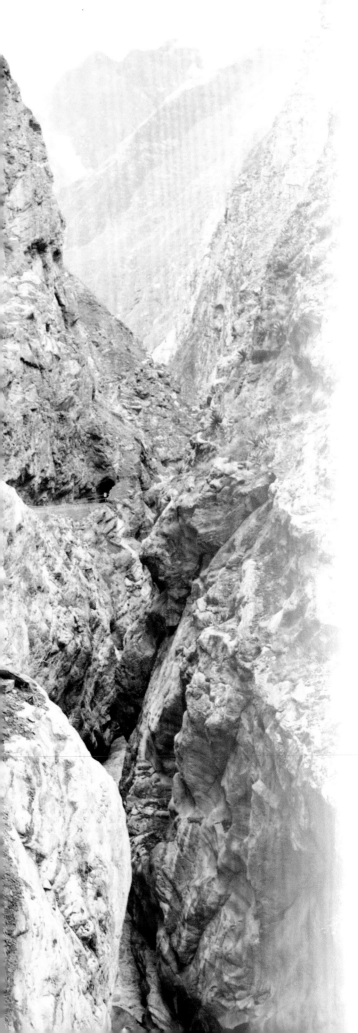

of a bus heading the other way. Coward that I am, I get on the throttle, hoping to force him to reverse, but the rusty coach keeps on coming until he is a couple of inches from my front bumper. I look in the rear-view mirror and see nothing but blackness. No choice. As I start to edge gingerly back, another bus appears from behind, blaring its horn and flashing. Typical. You wait ages for a bus, then two turn up at once to trap you in an Andean death tunnel. We sit in stalemate for a few minutes, both bus drivers honking and gesturing. What do you want me to do, señor? Eventually, Bus One starts to reverse. He inches back about 50 yards before pointing and waving to my left. Oh god. There is a car-sized window cut into the rock, looming out over the abyss below, with a sill of crumbling rock perhaps three feet across. He wants me to drive onto that ledge. I shake my head and cross my arms. Not happening. Bus Two begins to edge into the Duster's rear bumper, shoving me slowly but persistently into the gap. Happening, then. Head craned out the window, I edge into the too-small edge. When the Duster's left-front wheel is within two inches of the crumbly precipice, I stop. My bravery will permit me to go no further. Bus One lurches forward, convinced he can squeeze through. Alongside, mirrors folded, he must be within an inch of the Duster's flank. God, this is close. If he nudges us now, we will be over that edge and doing our best Wile E. Coyote impressions. And then dead. Inch by hideous inch, the bus edges past. Closer, closer... and then freedom. I tiptoe the Duster away from the ledge and out of the tunnel, not stopping to find out how the two buses passed each other. For all I know, they're still there now, locked in tunnelly stalemate for eternity.

Past the tunnels, beyond the abyss, into the lush mountain valley. And, finally, civilisation.

★★★★★

I do not know how there are not more dead dogs along Peru's roads. Conspicuously alive, the scruffy mutts are everywhere, hundreds in every tiny village, lounging under trucks or fighting lazily or, most often, trotting cheerily into the road in front of onrushing vehicles. (There are, officially, urban speed limits in Peru. They appear to be optional.) Stand at any Peruvian crossroads, and you'll witness the same scene played out every few minutes: dog

ambles into road in front of truck, truck squeals to a stop, miraculously avoiding flattening dog by about six inches, dog doesn't flinch, offers canine Gallic shrug to irate truck driver, continues across road. They never get hit. I can only conclude that Peruvian dogs are magic.

If the dogs don't scupper you, the mototaxis might. Three-wheeled scooters with a rough tarpaulin over the back to accommodate a couple of passengers, they weave manically across the road, hundreds of them in even the smallest town, criss-crossing in slow-motion orbit without regard for cars, road laws or mortality. Stopped for lunch in a street market, I watch a mototaxi laden with perhaps 50 car batteries wheeze up the gentlest of inclines at barely a mile an hour. Having progressed 20 yards in the best part of five minutes, the mototaxi's front wheel catches a pothole, jolting its body and sending a couple of dozen of the batteries scattering back down the street. Without so much as a flicker of annoyance, the driver climbs from his cab, slowly loads the batteries back onto the rear seat and resumes his glacial progress up the hill. ('What did you do today, darling?' 'Not much, dear. Became trapped in an infinite battery loop. You?')

An old lady under a huge, multi-hued hat is selling cute guinea pigs, perhaps a dozen of them in a bag by her feet. She holds one up and looks imploringly at me. So does the guinea pig.

'Sorry,' I grin though my best 'apologetic foreigner' face. 'Don't think they'd let me back on the plane with one of those.'

The old woman shakes her head sternly. 'Not plane,' she says. 'To eat now.' She makes a nibbling motion with her hands and mouth, as you'd munch a corn on the cob. Hot-buttered guinea pig. No wonder the little fella was looking desperate. Leaving fricasseed rodents to Peru's hardier lunchers, we cast off for the top of the world.

The summit of the Huinchas Pass stands 14,271 feet above sea level. There's a dizzying tarmac road to the top, but we're solemnly informed this is closed. (Either 'closed' or 'dead' – my Spanish isn't great.) So, demonstrating the do-or-almost-certainly-die mentality for which *TopGear* is famed, we are now heading for the top of Peru up a mud path that makes our earlier dirt road look like the M6 toll.

This place isn't so much off the beaten track as unaware of the existence of a beaten track. We wind higher and higher, over boulders and rockslides, through jungly ferns and cacti, past tiny villages of wood shacks and crumbling stone. Judging by the stares of the farmers we pass, we might be the first gringos to pass through this century. Stopping for photos, one tiny, wizened grandma becomes obsessed with my blue eyes, a situation I find quite charming until it becomes apparent she is seriously contemplating removing them from my face to keep as souvenirs.

Up, past knackered donkeys and more patchy dogs that snarl and nip at the Duster's tyres before retiring, wheezing, to the verge. And then nothing. No cars, no tarmac, no oxygen. Just mud, stones and vertigo-inducing drops. The cloud closes in. We are in darkest Peru, but there is no sign of a small, marmalade-hooked stuffed bear. (Yeah, Paddington Bear references. We totally went there.)

Over 13,000 feet, and the altitude sickness starts to hit hard. We have climbed from sea level almost three vertical miles in a single day. It's an odd, out-of-body sort of sickness: though you're acutely aware your movements are getting slower and your emotions less rational, there's nothing you can do about it. I spend two minutes attempting to locate reverse gear, which turns out to have been cunningly relocated exactly where it was before. This makes me very sad and I decide I should probably have a quick cry. It strikes me hazily this may not be the best mindset in which to tackle a deadly Andean ascent. The Duster, mountain goat that it is, soldiers on relentlessly. OK, so its idle has begun to wander a little, and I discover I have to dial in a load more revs to get going from stationary, but the little Dacia is coping with the lung-busting altitude far better than either

me or Matthias, whose face has assumed the colour of absinthe and who is making the sort of respiratory noises commonly associated with advanced lung disease.

Higher and higher and the scenery turns curiously familiar. Granite outcrops and blue-green grass, a psychotropic interpretation of the Scottish Highlands. As we crest 14,000 feet – a mile above even the tallest Alpine pass – we break through the cloudline, and the Andes roll out about us, perfect snow-capped peaks poking through the mist like volcanic islands. The setting sun turns the fog below into a sea of trippy purple-pink. In celebration, I drive 500 yards up a scree field to the top of an Ande. The Duster has made it to the ceiling of Peru.

Traditionally, this is where the story should end: the humble car gloriously conquering one of the world's toughest climates. But, as Felix Baumgartner will attest, what goes up must come down, and so must we.

★★★★★

It is deep darkness as we begin the descent to Caraz, the nearest town. The tarmac road is now open. This proves to be A Bad Thing. The tarmac road turns out to be a track barely a lane wide, hacked into the side of a cliff, covered in a film of gravelly dust, devoid of markings or barriers. Below my left shoulder twinkle Caraz's lights, over a mile straight down. If we slide off the road, that's what we're hitting.

What follows is the most nerve-wracking hour of my life. Not that rollercoasterish oh-God-I'm-about-to-die-oh-no-I'm-alive-hahaha sort of fear, the sort quick-hit adrenaline addicts seek out, but a fear far more unpleasant and pervasive, the knowledge that the merest brush of the wrong pedal, a fractional misjudgement of steering, a misreading of the road, will result in plummety death. Hairpins are the worst, steering into empty darkness, no point on the road on which to fix your aim.

We are, it strikes me, putting a lot of trust in the Romanian men who checked the Duster's brake hoses, who fitted its wiring. If anything goes even marginally wrong now – flat tyre, power steering glitch, headlight fuse failure – we are dead in the most horribly inevitable way possible. But the Duster keeps on, unstoppable, unruffled, its mud-painted headlights throwing a narrow,

dim beam on the narrow, dim road. I decide, altitude-drunk, thankful to be alive, that this must be the perfect car for Peru. You want something with four-wheel drive, something cheap enough you won't mind it getting a bit dented by, say, a rapidly onrushing valley floor. Decent visibility is a must, to avoid clouting a mototaxi and being clouted by a ten-tonne truck.

And, the altitude-monologue continues, all those things that make the Duster so good here make it the perfect cheap car for Britain. A bit of extra suspension travel isn't only useful when you're tackling an Ande – it provides useful compliance on crumbled tarmac too, absorbing divots and ruts. The trade-off – in budget cars, at least – is usually a wallowing, sailboat approach to corners. But the Duster is slop-free. Maybe it's the hypoxia speaking, but I'm pretty sure it nails the ride – handling balance better than cars at many times its price.

The Duster doesn't aspire to budget chic or any such daft notion. It's simply budget, and all the better for it: honest, simple, good enough to make you reassess what you actually *need*, not want, from a new car. I can't claim it steers like an Exige or has a gearshift to match the Boxster, but it does all that stuff entirely adequately. And OK, its interior won't send Laurence Llewelyn-Bowen into raptures, but it has everything you need: seats, steering wheel, radio, all still attached after our thousand-mile off-road battering. We have subjected this simple, brilliant little car to punishment beyond anything that even Britain's most abused Land Rover has endured, and it has passed with flying colours. Brownish colours, admittedly, but flying brownish colours nonetheless.

Altitude sickness promotes grand, woozy thoughts, and this is mine. The Duster distills the very essence of motoring. Some cars we love for their pupil-melting beauty or for pushing the boundaries of technical possibility. But the main reason we love cars is because they offer freedom, a passport to the furthest-flung corners of the globe. And no car in the world offers more freedom for your quid than the soft, strong and thoroughly canyon-proof Dacia Duster.

Better look elsewhere for lunch, vultures.

UP FOR A PINT

TOPGEAR DRIVES TO THE MOUNTAIN KINGDOM OF LESOTHO FOR A SWIFT ONE IN AFRICA'S HIGHEST PUB. BECAUSE... WELL, WHY NOT?

Welcome to no-man's land, population zero. We exited South Africa at the base of the Sani Pass, the border post no more than a couple of Nissen huts and a barbed-wire fence strung across the hillside. Passports stamped, gate slammed behind the Range Rover Sport, and now we are in no-man's land. The Lesotho border lies at the top of the pass, a thousand metres straight up and 20 miles along the track. We're stranded in the space between countries.

My first thought is the only logical one when you find yourself abandoned in a place without laws: so this means we can drive as fast as we want, right?

Turns out to be a moot point. Yes, I am loose with a 288bhp RRS in the land that traffic police forgot, but I'm also on a road impossible to tackle at more than 20mph:

rutted rock and gravel, tight hairpins and thousand-foot drops off the barrierless edges. Potential for non-speeding-based crime, too, is limited, there being no one, literally *no one* around to be criminal toward.

Utter emptiness aside, as no-man's lands go, this one hardly feels the most foreboding. In fact, on a sunny late-spring morning, the bottom of the Sani Pass is surely as idyllic a spot as exists on the planet. The grassy uplands of the Drakensberg Mountains, green and glossy as velvet, fringe the horizon. Birds sing, gentle streams of meltwater trickle across the road as near-vertical basalt peaks loom a mile above. A vervet monkey scurries up a purple jacaranda tree. It's like *Jurassic Park* without the ravenous raptors or Dickie Attenborough.

I crane my neck upwards. The top of the escarpment,

WHERE IS IT?
South Africa, sort of

WHICH BIT?
The road between Underberg and Mokhotlong

GIVE ME CO-ORDINATES!
-29.588143, 29.294267

WHEN SHOULD I GO?
It's bleak up here, but probably most pleasant from September to March

HOW LONG WILL IT TAKE?
At least two days

HOW DO I GET THERE?
Fly to Durban and drive west

WHAT'S THE WEATHER LIKE?
Disturbing

WHAT'S THE ROAD LIKE?
Loose and brown

WHAT IF I GET LOST?
They have maps and road signs and everything. Failing that, ask a local from a safe distance

TG TOP TIP:
Call 10111 for help. If there's no signal, it was nice knowing you...

ONE MORE THING:
Beware of the local brew. If that doesn't get you, the altitude sickness will

some 3,000 metres above sea level, marks the end of no-man's land: the frontier of the kingdom of Lesotho. That's where we're aiming.

Why? Because of history, that's why. The Sani Pass, one of Africa's most notorious mountain roads, was employed for hundreds of years as a bridle path along which mules and horses would ferry goods between what we now call South Africa and southern Lesotho. It remained impassable to vehicles until 1948, when a budding entrepreneur called David Alexander conquered the Sani in his troupe of imported 4x4s, among the very first cars built by little-known British upstart Land Rover. In seven years, Alexander and his Series Is tamed the Sani, turning this muddy donkey track into a muddy car track. Land Rover made the Sani, and the Sani made Land Rover.

But there's a far more important reason for our voyage to the faraway kingdom. Beer. Lesotho is home to the self-appointed Highest Pub In Africa. As the two pubs nearest to the *TG* office are shoo-ins for the titles of Most Expensive Pub in Britain and Fightiest Pub in the Northern Hemisphere, we figured it'd be good to get a third superlative to complete the set.

Gotta get there first, though. As we scale the pass, KwaZulu-Natal falls away beneath us, and the path turns twistier, slippier and nastier. Click the RRS into mud-and-ruts programme, engage low-range mode on the gearbox. The Sport rises on its springs, flashes up a cheery array of lights and twisty-axle graphics on the dash, and sets about trudging its way up the one-in-two rocky scree with the effortless plod of a packhorse. No scrabble, no

MOKHOTLONG

Drakensburg
Mountains

Mkhomazi
Wilderness
Area

Himeville

UNDERBERG

LEFT: *Up here, the wind is strong enough to peel your face. Best to stay in the sanctuary of the car.*

FAR RIGHT (OPPOSITE PAGE): *The Range Rover Sport – master of all landscapes, and relentless in its pursuit of a cold pint of lager.*

BELOW: *The tallest peak around here stands at 3,482m. That's triple Snowdon's height. And there's not even a railway for lazy people!*

slip, just a relentless, oddly delicate assault. And this from a car on summer road tyres and 21-inch wheels. So assured is the Sport's gentle ascent that I decide this is a good moment to take my hands from the wheel and dive into the footwell to retrieve a chunk of biltong dropped earlier. When I resurface a few seconds later, I note with interest that a) we are a couple of metres from toppling off the pass and down the side of a mountain and b) the photographer is capable of emitting noises at the outer reaches of the human aural register. Mental note. RRS: very good at off-roading; cannot steer itself.

Approaching from the south, you can see nothing of Lesotho until you're almost in it. The last hundred metres through no-man's land are a scrabble up an almost vertical cliff face, hopping over rockfalls and collapsed road. Were a Bond villain to design his own no-expense-spared mountain lair, I'm not sure he could come up with a driveway more imposing than this.

A weird driveway for a weird country. Lesotho is, essentially, an island nation, but one surrounded by near-impassable cliff rather than sea. It's a statistical anomaly of a place: the same size as Belgium, it's the only country

in the world to lie entirely above 1,000m in altitude. In fact, Lesotho's lowest point is 1,400m above sea level, which is the highest lowest point of any country on earth. It's the most southerly landlocked country in the world, and one of just three countries to be completely enclaved within just one other: the Vatican City and San Marino are the other two. Two turns from the top, I've no idea what to expect.

The end of days, that's what. As we roll over the top of the pass, Africa's palette shifts in an instant from the aquamarine of a lush valley morning to the black-grey of a post-nuclear winter. Dark, doom-laden clouds close about us and a 70mph wind whips down from the north, spitting grit into our eyes. Photographer Brimble, hopping out to take a photo, has to grab a doorhandle to avoid being blown off the edge and back down into South Africa.

Through the Lesotho border post – a rusted shack and twist of wire that makes the South African effort at the bottom look like Fort Knox – and into a different century. We are faced with the most un-African of vistas, a post-apocalyptic interpretation of the remotest sweeps

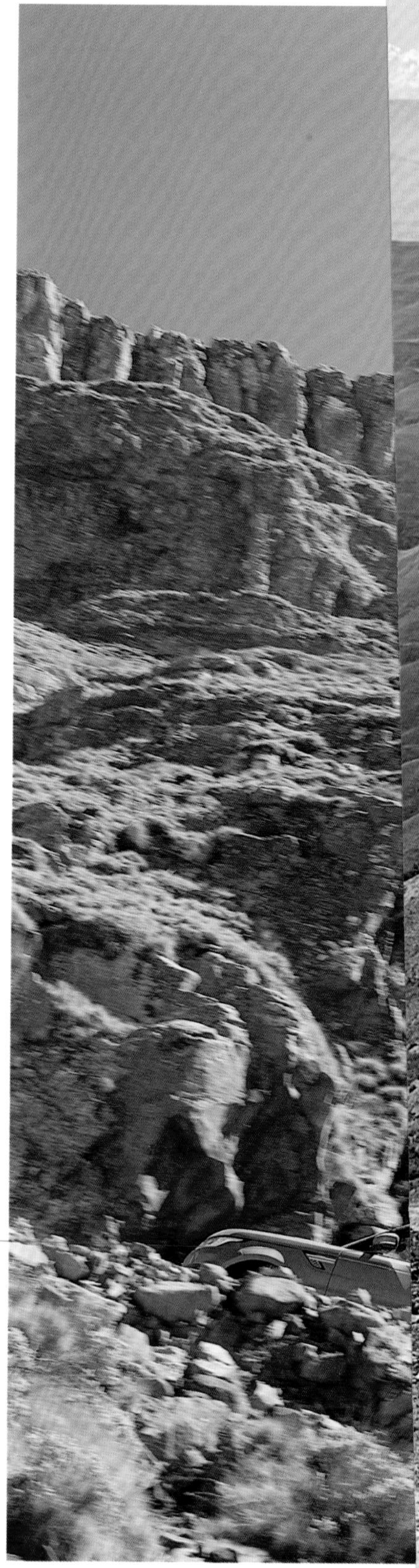

of Dartmoor: wild, wind-whipped moorland as far as the eye can see, with a rough stone path stretching off into the distance. There is not a tree in sight – we're two miles above sea level, way up above the tree line – just a bleak ocean of scrubby moorland and boulders. The air is thin, watered-down, leaving us gasping for breath like a pensioner with an 80-a-day habit. The Sport doesn't care, rolling calmly on.

Slowly, lumpily, we wind north into the heart of Lesotho. There are no towns, no villages visible in any direction, just the odd cluster of stone huts huddled into the hillsides. God, they must be cold places to live. Triple-glazing and underfloor heating, I fear, are yet to become de rigueur in these parts.

A shepherd trots towards us on a stumpy horse, driving his dozen sheep down the track in close-knit four-by-three formation. I am impressed by their synchronised obedience, and then realise they're desperately clustered together for warmth. Their owner is wrapped head to toe in a vast poncho, only his eyes visible within the mass of wool. I click up the Sport's heated seats a couple of notches and feel like the worst sort of tourist.

The local Basotho are known as the blanket people, on account of, erm, the fact they wear a lot of blankets. If you spent your life in snowy, sub-zero temperatures – Lesotho is one of only two countries in sub-Saharan Africa in which you can ski (though apparently the vin chaud is frightfully average, dahling) – you'd opt for a blanket-based wardrobe, too. I wonder what made the Basotho leave the clement plains and thick, syrupy air of South Africa below and venture up to this harsh, unyielding land. The reason, I discover later, is that, some 200 years ago, the Basotho became rather bored of being butchered by the Zulu. Anything for a bit of peace and quiet.

As we ford a shallow river, a steatopygous momma materialises from behind a drystone wall, blankets whipping in the wind. She waves urgently at us. I lower the window.

'You are... so pretty!' she exclaims in precise, slow English.

'Thanks!' I reply, a little bewildered. 'You're very pretty too.'

She nods and smiles. 'You are... very big.'

The Basotho are not a tall race, but then again, neither am I. I begin to suspect something may be getting lost in translation.

'Very big... and very fast. I like you.
Ah.

As the sun drops, the black clouds li
Lesotho reveals itself to be, in a desolate
oddly beautiful. Unlike its roads, wh
before, raise their game to deeply harr
Sport seems unperturbed. Heading no
to the Sani this morning, we trailed a L
being driven *keenly* along a twisty, swe
the Disco – admittedly a porker in th
SUVS – tilted and lurched its way rou
bends, our Sport remained perfectly

ANTARCTICA / ACROSS THE SOUTH POLE

DISTANCE: 2,500 MILES

CAR: CATERPILLAR D6N

THE COLDEST JOURNEY

IN 2013, RICHMOND DYKES FILED THIS REPORT FROM WHAT AMOUNTED TO A VERY POSH TENT ON THE CONTINENT OF ANTARCTICA – ONE OF THE WORLD'S HARSHEST, BLEAKEST AND LEAST-FORGIVING ENVIRONMENTS. WHY WAS HE THERE? ALLOW HIM TO EXPLAIN...

The idea to cross Antarctica in winter was conceived in 2008 when Sir Ranulph Fiennes and Dr Mike Stroud came up with a plan to cross the continent – alone and on foot – in the southern winter months. This is something no human being has ever managed before, and is an adventure of mind-boggling physical and mental extremity.

There's just one, small problem: in winter, in Antarctica, the weather is so extreme that there is literally no chance of rescue or aid, should something bad happen. You're on your own. Which meant that, after a long discussion with the Foreign Office, Sir Ranulph was only issued a permit to attempt the crossing unsupported if he could carry all the provisions required for a winter crossing. Which is where we come in.

After gaining the necessary permissions, Sir Ran and his team started to search for a suitable vehicle to pull a mobile landtrain across Antarctica. This would need to carry all the food, medical supplies, science equipment and fuel required to sustain the expedition during a harsh Antarctic winter, when temperatures can drop to as low as -90°C. Which is as difficult as it sounds.

www.seeingisbelieving.org

could to be entirely self-sufficient for what might be the next 12 months.

The next morning was busy, and the following day we moved up the hill and made camp for the final stages of our ice-train tests, practising towing the whole setup. It was only when we started the first pull of the complete ice-train that I realised how slow the trip was going to be; we'd be travelling at a speed that would frustrate even James May. As I write, we are currently two days into the fuel-drop trip and have covered 57 kilometres. But there's big stuff ahead, and I doubt I'll get much chance to be lazy during the next few months…

Shortly after this article appeared in the March, 2013 issue of *TopGear* magazine, Sir Ranulph was forced to abandon the trip due to severe frostbite. The rest of the team soldiered on, but had to turn back when they encountered an impassable, 100km crevasse field. Despite not reaching the final destination, they continued their good work by spending the remainder of the expedition on scientific research.

FAR LEFT (OPPOSITE PAGE): *Saga's Mediterranean cruise had taken a horrible detour. And is that man's head stuck in a bulldozer? Fetch an ambulance!*

LEFT: *Hard hats: essential survival gear in the harshest environment on earth. Best of, chappies. bring us back a penguin, will you?*

BELOW: *Beware of giant cracks. At best you'll have to turn back. At worst you'll be swallowed and never seen again.*

which can be unfurled to enable repairs in bad weather – a mobile garage, if you like.

The final preparation took place during late 2012, with the Finning team putting in extremely long hours on both machines to get them ready to be shipped down to Antarctica on the *SA Agulhas*, a special ice-strengthened ship and former polar exploration vessel. Once the Cats were safely on their way, Spencer, I and the rest of the Ice Team flew out to meet the *Agulhas* in Cape Town, before making our way down to the Antarctic ice shelf where unloading would take place.

We arrived at the head of the Crown Bay inlet the day after we started forcing our way through the floes, but had to wait for another three days while the ice cleared enough for us to crunch our way right up to the Antarctic ice shelf. Once we had managed to secure a position, we had to work quickly. The ship's crane fired up and unloaded one of the sledges and the science caboose – this allowed us to check the condition of the ice until we were given the signal to lift Rover and Seeker from number-two hold and get them onto the ground.

We hadn't been allowed down into the hold to start the engines on the Cats while we were at sea because we were carrying several hundred tonnes of highly explosive fuel in the same hold. But now we could access the area, Spencer and I went down to change a few filters – after their sitting for over a month without being started, we didn't want to take any chances. Then we checked all the oil levels, crossed our fingers and fired up the engines. Soon, the Cats were hooked up to the crane and lifted into the Antarctic sunshine.

As soon as the 'dozers were safely deposited on the ice, I clambered over the bow and down the ladder onto the ice shelf for the first time. And there I was, driving in Antarctica, when suddenly it hit home that although the doors were open and I had the escape hatch, if this thing broke through the ice, it was game over.

Thankfully the surface held firm as I tracked up to safer and thicker ground, where we could start our preparations and put our machines to work for the first time. From then on, daily duties consisted of shuttling fuel and supplies up to the top loading area for storage, until we could move the science and living caboose up the hill to the top staging point. There was a lot to do until we

WHERE IS IT?
Do you have a globe? Turn it upside down. There.

WHICH BIT?
Right across the south pole

GIVE ME CO-ORDINATES!
-71.962459, 23.335728

WHEN SHOULD I GO?
Nobody has ever crossed Antarctica in winter, so there's history to be made…

HOW LONG WILL IT TAKE?
We'd give it a year

HOW DO I GET THERE?
From Cape Town, simply board an icebreaker to Crown Bay where you can unload your bulldozer

WHAT'S THE WEATHER LIKE?
Murderous

WHAT'S THE ROAD LIKE?
Crevassey

WHAT IF I GET LOST?
Beyond Princess Elisabeth Station you're on your own, as rescue missions are impossible

TG TOP TIP:
In winter, most of the trip will be in darkness and temperatures will reach −80 °C. So pack some mittens

ONE MORE THING:
To qualify for a winter crossing, make sure you're done by the September equinox. Good luck!

The team looked at various types of machinery from around the globe, and eventually settled on Caterpillar bulldozers. An approach was made to Finning, the world's largest Caterpillar dealership, and after lengthy discussions about which type of machine would be most suitable for the job, it was decided that a pair of Caterpillar D6Ns would be just the thing. The bulldozers themselves were the Goldilocks option: not too big, not too small… just about perfect.

But while these machines are tough in every respect, we couldn't take chances. Knowing where they would be going and what they would be subjected to, the Finning team was tasked with the job of fitting a pair of D6Ns with copious extras. As a result, the two bulldozers – nicknamed Rover and Seeker – are now the only vehicles in the world to have fully customised Antarctic options.

Probably the most important of these are the crevasse arms, which will stop us falling completely into big cracks in the ice. They also double up as crane and attachment points for the ground-penetrating radar, a system to help us figure out where the crevasses are. Quite useful if you don't want to find yourself upside down in a very big hole in the middle of nowhere…

Other extras include hydraulically driven generators, which will supply 'free' electricity to the living and science accommodation cabooses that will be dragged behind us. There are also heating pads fitted to the engines, transmission and hydraulic tanks, helping to keep the hearts of the Cat D6Ns warm, and roof canopies

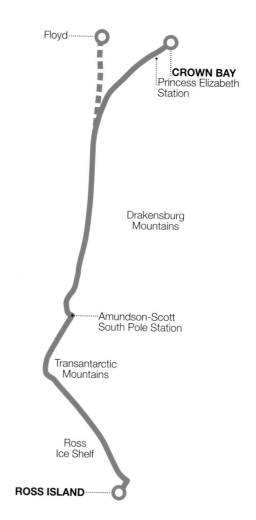

Floyd

CROWN BAY
Princess Elizabeth Station

Drakensburg Mountains

Amundson-Scott South Pole Station

Transantarctic Mountains

Ross Ice Shelf

ROSS ISLAND

SURVIVAL CAPSULE

WELCOME TO NAMIBIA, WHERE CARS AREN'T CARS... THEY'RE LIFE SUPPORT MACHINES

Blasting dustily down a dirt road in the vast, deserted badlands of southern Namibia, the Amarok's temperature gauge is reading 54.5°C. In old money, that's 130°F. It's also, as meat enthusiasts will attest, the temperature at the centre of a medium-rare steak. So if we, photographer Wycherley and I, were to become separated from the Amarok now, within a few hours we would, quite literally, be cooked through. Cooked, delicious, and eventually eaten by zebras.

Bumping along at, ahem, enthusiastic speeds, coolly cocooned within the Amarok's air-conditioned cabin, I wonder if its temp gauge might be exaggerating. I lower the driver's window, and am punched hard in the side of the head by a slug of brutal, dry heat, a fan-oven blast that sucks the moisture from my eyeballs and leaves me wheezing. I rapidly raise the window and conclude the Amarok is not exaggerating. Breaking down now would definitely equal lightly browned, charbroiled death.

Sure as hell no chance of a human finding us before we reached perfectly seared, pink-centred edibleness. We haven't seen another car, another soul, for six hours. The last scrubby shack (deserted) we passed was 80 miles back, the last shop (closed) 100 miles before that. What do people here do if they want, y'know, stuff? 'Just popping out for some milk, darling. See you in September.'

Phone for help? Not a chance. There's no mobile phone signal here: even if there were, what would you tell the rescue services? 'Hi, Namibian RAC? We've broken down. Badly. Where are we? Er, Namibia? More

WHERE IS IT?
Africa. Bottom left

WHICH BIT?
From Kotzenshoop to Oranjemund via Fish Canyon

GIVE ME CO-ORDINATES!
-27.702838, 17.611085

WHEN SHOULD I GO?
There are over 300 days of sunshine, so pick a cool(ish) one between June and August

HOW LONG WILL IT TAKE?
Nine hours if you don't stop, twice that if you do

HOW DO I GET THERE?
You could drive up from Cape Town, or grab an internal flight to Oranjemund

WHAT'S THE WEATHER LIKE?
Melty

WHAT'S THE ROAD LIKE?
Sandy

WHAT IF I GET LOST?
This is a land without signposts, so pack a compass or follow the stars

TG TOP TIP:
Carry many supplies, both for yourself and your car. Or else you'll both be very thirsty and possibly a bit dead

ONE MORE THING:
Unless you are the lovechild of Ray Mears and Bear Grylls, you should probably hire a guide

specifically? No idea, sorry. I can see… sand. And rocks.' There are no towns here, few signposts. And if your car has any propensity towards mechanical failure, these roads will find it: loose-dirt tracks that veer in an instant from thick sand to rock-hard corrugation, with nausea-inducing humpbacks and dog-sized boulders thrown in for good measure.

Welcome to Africa. The final frontier for carmakers. If you want to conquer the toughest of the inhabited continents, this is what your vehicles have to survive. If, specifically, you're VW, this is what your shiny pickup has to survive to overhaul Toyota as king of Africa. Europe's biggest auto maker is quietly taking over China, and South America too. But rural Africa is a rather slower nut to crack.

Cars aren't a luxury here, a convenient alternative to catching the train or slipping into the Lycra for a bracing cycle. They are quite literally lifelines. Even in the wildest corners of the Scottish Highlands, if your car breaks down it'll be, at most, a matter of hours until someone passes. Not days. Certainly not weeks. But if your engine goes bang in the middle of the desert, you will become a) dead and b) medium-rare.

Which means that – outside the big cities, at least – the car world's relentless march of fashion, of newness and of technology all counts for bugger-all. Stop-start? Active suspension? Just another thing to break. Forget traffic alerts or DAB radio. Out here, reliability and indestructibility are all.

Gondwana
Nature Park

Richtersveld
National Park

FISH CANYON

Aussenkehr
Nature
Reserve

Richtersveld
World Heritage
Site

KOTZENSHOOP

ORANJEMUND

LEFT: *In 600 miles, make a slight left turn. Only kidding. There's no turn. And no road signs, either…'*

BELOW: *Is it a Mars Rover, or shiny new Volswagen pickup on some big stones in Africa? You decide!*

RIGHT: *Average annual rainfall? About 20mm. Pack water. And more water. Or else you'll be eaten by murder zebras.*

That's why Africa is Toyota country. Since the sixties, the continent has been dominated by, first, the FJ – Japan's bare-bones answer to the Series 1 Land Rover, as driven by Hammond in Bolivia on *Top Gear* TV – and latterly the Hilux. Why? Because they simply refuse to break. All those tests that inspired *TopGear* to declare the Hilux the Most Indestructible Car in the History of Ever – the fact it'll keep going whether drowned, burned or crushed under hundreds of tonnes of rubble – are exactly why Africa loves it so, why 40-year-old examples are still creaking round the deserts, savannahs and jungles after a lifetime's abuse.

However, even the modern Hilux is far from luxurious. It's a great, gruff rhino of a thing, roaring lustily on the move, its utilitarian cabin designed to be wipe-clean in the event of, say, having to bludgeon a bloodthirsty leopard to death against the steering wheel.

Enter VW. The Amarok, hopes Wolfsburg, can bring a soupçon of car-like sophistication to a sector that regards digital clocks and electric windows as a bit nouveau. It's available with Volkswagen's quietest diesels and a posh eight-speed auto 'box, as well as the firm's full road-car options list. It's quiet and passably sophisticated, holding pace on motorways without reducing your ears to pulp. Nice in theory, but quietness and posh kit counts for nothing in wildest Namibia unless the pickup they're stuck to can survive a particularly nasty apocalypse. Prove you can take a beating, VW, then we'll admire your smart leather and dual-zone climate control.

Which is why we have spent a week in one of Africa's harshest corners, diligently trying to smash an Amarok to pieces. So far we have failed. This is not for want of trying. Short of tipping it off a cliff or getting dictatorial on it with a Kalashnikov, we have done everything in our power to break this pickup. Yesterday, I drove up the side of a 1-in-1 rubble canyon wall, breadknife-edged stones pinging off the tyres and clattering into the Amarok's underbody. This morning, I dropped it 500 feet down a near-vertical sand dune and squealed like a trapped pig all the way to the bottom. The Amarok handled both with unblinking, camel-like resilience. Sand, cliffs, rock fields, the Amarok has devoured the lot, and all on standard, fully inflated road tyres. I am begrudgingly impressed.

And, between the boulder-scrambling and the dune-sliding, thousands of miles of the sort of slippery, bumpy track we're piling along now, vapour trails of dust billowing a mile behind our truck.

Tackling these roads at a decent lick is not a relaxing job. The cambered surface shifts second by second, deeper sand dragging the wheels off the road, hard ruts bouncing the tyres from the ground. Just to make things interesting, a 50mph crosswind whips sand across the road and batters the Amarok's bluff body. Feel the grip shifting from tyre to tyre, gently coax the truck back into line, don't jerk the wheel. Most importantly, don't crash.

In truth, I'm not exactly sure what the legal speed limit is here. It seems a little irrelevant. On these roads, the factor limiting your speed isn't avoiding licence points, but a desire for self-preservation. No chance of another car springing up on you: you can see vehicles coming the other way from 10 miles off, kicking dust plumes high into the air. Humans? Not for a few hundred miles in any direction. If you get it wrong – sneeze and veer off the road, catch a rogue rock – you'll flip for a few hundred yards, and then you'll die. I've no idea what adrenaline and skill is required to wrestle an F1 car on a hot lap, but I can't imagine it's a patch on piloting a sensible diesel pickup down a straight African road.

On the subject of diesel, our Amarok has a good 'un – VW's 2.0-litre 4cyl turbo making 178bhp and a chunky 309lb ft of torque. You'd never mistake it for a silky BMW six, but by the standards of ute engines, it's a muted, smooth thing – and, most importantly, seemingly unflustered by its 50°C roasting. A four-pot turbodiesel might sound pretty workaday in Britain, but down here it's regarded as almost radical. Stopped for fuel a few days back in Kotzenshoop, right on the South African border, a couple of locals – both pink of face and khaki of attire – wandered over to peruse our pickup.

'Amarok,' grunted the bigger, more ham-like of the two, looking at the badge. He boasted a seventies moustache and a strong Afrikaans accent, which makes even the most innocent utterance sound like you're trying to start a fight. 'Turbo, eh?'

Before I could answer in the affirmative, the pinker, marginally less ham-like khaki-wearer interjected aggressively. 'And wha's wrong with that?' He had,

implausibly, a Scottish accent flecked with a hint of Afrikaans, which is precisely as weird as you might imagine. He gestured towards his battered Land Rover Defender 110, every panel of which appeared to have sustained a significant but very localised accident. 'She's got a turbo, and she's gone half a million kilometres, no problems.'

'Stresses the engine,' replied Hamface authoritatively. 'And can you fix it when it goes wrong?' He wafted a sausage-like arm at his faded, double-cab Hilux, so dented it made the Defender look showroom-fresh. 'No turbo on that, 750,000km, tight as a duck's arse.' Few great romantic poems have been written in Afrikaans.

'Aye, and what sort of consumption d'ye get from that?' snorted Afriscotsman. 'Two point seven, is it? Lucky to get 15 to the gallon from that. Landie'll get mid-twenties, easy. That's the problem with you Toyota lot. You're *proud* of shite consumption. What are you gonna do when you run out of fuel in the middle o' nowhere? That's the difference between life and death, that is…'

Leaving the khaki crew to their tiff, I snuck off to buy gallons of drinking water and a few kilos of biltong, a tough, jerky-like southern African snack made from the meat of cows raised exclusively on a diet of Jeremy Kyle reruns and *Daily Mail* comment pieces. When I tiptoed past 10 minutes later, they were still going strong.

Probably a good thing I didn't mention our Amarok was packing not only a faddish turbodiesel but, even worse, an automatic gearbox. A fine one, too: the 8spd ZF – a transmission we've already seen and admired in the Touareg, Phaeton and others – is as good as torque-converters get, shifting almost telepathically and refusing to be caught out on even the gnarliest boulder-crawls or dune-blasts. Adding complication to a desert-bashing pickup might seem a recipe for disaster, but VW says the auto 'box actually adds, er, simplicity: because eight ratios can cover such a wide spread, it negates the need for a low-range 'box. Apparently, the 'box has just five moving parts (which surely doesn't seem enough), and, because it can keep the diesel in its sweet spot, reduces wear on the engine. Here's hoping. I don't fancy starring as the bloated, vulture-pecked carcass in the next David Attenborough documentary.

At least you're unlikely to be savaged by lions or leopards out here. Such a barren, lifeless landscape can't support enough prey to keep a big predator well fed, so

Africa's largest, toothiest man-eaters tend to stick to the fertile savannah. Even so, a smattering of wild horses, springbok and zebra wander the canyons, and however peaceable the stripy-pyjama-wearing horses might look, I've a sneaking suspicion that, faced with the choice of crunching through a sand dune of desiccated spiny shrubs or a plump, juicy Englishman, they'd rapidly ditch their long-held vegetarianism.

Beware, too, the kudu. The kudu is a large, well-built deer with twisted, razor-tipped horns a metre and a half in length. A male kudu can weigh nearly 300kg, with all its weight balanced at windscreen height atop a set of long, spindly legs. As you may have guessed, you do not want to hit a kudu. Local wisdom dictates there are two strategies for avoiding this. It's not simply a case of keeping your eyes peeled, because kudu are a) impressively camouflaged, b) very fast and c) easily spooked by cars, meaning they have a nasty habit of bolting from nowhere across the road in front of you. Strategy One is to drive very slowly, making sure you have enough time to brake to a complete stop, should a kudu jump out in front of you. On dirt tracks, this means limiting yourself to about 20mph. Everywhere. Strategy Two is to drive as fast as possible and hope you're past the kudu before it decides to bolt across the road. *TopGear*, predictably, has adopted Strategy Two.

The problem with Strategy Two is that it does kick up rather a lot of dust. Fine as flour, the stuff gets everywhere, wedging its way into any nook or crevice, binding with any moisture to create gummy, grating paste. And I'm not just talking about on the car: the dust finds its way into corners of your body you didn't think could possibly get dusty. I'm sensing I should leave it at that.

Between the scalding sun, the invasive dust, the dead earth, it's tough to imagine how humans survive here. But they do, clinging onto existence in this harshest of landscapes. Yesterday, we passed through a scrubby settlement, a higgle-piggle of – what? – two or three thousand tiny reed huts perched against a scorched, dusty hillside. Hardly even huts, most of them, just flimsy windbreaks, a crude screen to keep the worst of the sun out. No running water, no sanitation, just basket-huts and a few tin-shack shops – including, most interestingly, the 'LIVING2GETHER BAR AND DRIVING SCHOOL', unquestionably the most dangerous dual-function establishment since Barry's Firearm and Magic Mushroom Mart.

I got chatting to a teenager called Albertus Seister. I know this is how his name is spelt, because he wrote it down and ordered me to mention him. Albertus told me – matter-of-factly as reciting a bus timetable – that his parents had both died, and he was supporting his sisters by collecting waste paper from around the town for a dollar or two a day. He regarded himself as one of the lucky ones, because he had a job. I know you don't come to *TopGear* for your annual dose of social reality, but it'd be remiss not to note that when we talk about selling cars in Africa, we're referring to the tiny, mainly white minority who can dream of affording a new one. Most of the trucks on the roads here trickle down through the system over years, even decades. Put it this way: it'll be a long time before anyone in that town will be driving an Amarok.

But will the big VW still be going in the 2030s, clattering along with a seven-figure score on its odometer? I'd put money on it. A week of patented *TG* pounding across even the harshest desert can't replicate 20 years and half a million miles of abuse at the hands of Namibian farmers, but this thing feels as indestructible as they come, capable of surviving whatever the continent can throw at it. Of course, not all of Africa is as dry and desolate as southern Namibia, but this is true of much of it: the roads are harsh and occasionally non-existent, and if you break down, it'll take the AA a very long time to find you.

The Amarok seems up to the challenge. As it slithers up a long, dusty incline, it occurs to me how very good cars are at... surviving. Especially big, no-nonsense pickups like this one. Much better than humans, certainly. Stick a pickup in 50 heat or -20cold, and it'll soldier on regardless. A human will rapidly become cooked/frozen.

Over the rise, and from nowhere, the most astonishing vista unfurls before us: a monstrous, half-mile-wide chasm slashed straight across the landscape, dropping 500 metres vertically to a snaking river below. This is, I discover later, the Fish River Canyon, the world's second largest after the Grand Canyon. There are no signs, no noticeboards, no warning you're about to plummet into one of the world's natural wonders, or even that it's there. I like that. You're on your own out here. Want to survive? Better make sure your car's up to it. And watch out for the MurderZebras.

lane in each direction, with trucks and road trains kissing wing mirrors as they pass. The autobahn is well lit, too. While street lights on the Stuart Highway arrive only when it passes through a microscopic township, of which there are exactly two: the bustling business district of Ti Tree, which 157 people call home, and the somewhat sleepier Aileron, with its seven residents.

One of those seven people is Greg Dick, who has run the Aileron Roadhouse for the past 30 years, and who so perfectly encapsulates the NT residents' reaction to the speed issue he should run for mayor. Dick, for the record, has a pet wedge-tailed eagle, a gigantic, predatory bird with a wingspan of more than six feet. Passing tourists loved it. Until it ate one of their dogs.

'Mate, we couldn't give a s**t. I was driving at 180kph [112mph] when there was no speed limit, and I was driving at 180kph when there was a speed limit. The only difference is that now I don't need to slow down if I think I see a cop,' he says.

'It's all you blokes who make a big deal out of it. It's normal for us out here.'

It's a feeling that's echoed by the few people we stumble across as we traipse up and down the derestricted zone. Locals like John Farrell, who arrived in the Northern Territory in the seventies for a two-week holiday and kind of forgot to leave. John is part of a mass-scale road-improvement project that'll see a little more than A$3m spent on making the derestricted zone safer.

'It's excellent. There's something great about coming up on a police car sitting on 150kph [93mph] and overtaking them. Now that's a fun feeling,' he says.

'But at the end of the day, it's the fatigue that gets you out here. That or the critters…'

We arrive two weeks after the speed limit was removed, and already a legend has formed in the sleepy townships. A story passed on in the roadside truck stops and petrol stations: did you hear about the bloke who clipped 275kph (170mph) in his Aston Martin V8 Vantage? Turns out that of all the supercar-driving visitors who descended on this usually quiet stretch of road, this chap had set the record. And just like that, we have a target in our sights. In the interests of road safety, of course.

We line up at our predetermined starting grid, framed

SOUTH AMERICA

DISTANCE: 504 MILES

CAR: Toyota Land Cruiser, Range
Rover Classic, Suzuki SJ413

TOP GEAR TELLY TRIP: BOLIVIA TO CHILE

'I'm now all on my own on
Death Road. I have no idea
where Ray Mears and Ted
Nugent are. They could be
dead.' Clarkson

'Apart from James driving
into a village well, we made
good progress towards the
Chilean border...' Clarkson

COROICO

Nuestra Señora de La Paz

Calamarca

Patacamaya

Callapa

Arica · · · · · Parque Nacional Lauca

Parque Nacional Volcán Isluga

IQUIQUE · · · · · Huara

your turn!

WHERE IS IT?
Underneath North America

WHICH BIT?
From Coroico in Bolivia to Iquique in Chile

GIVE ME CO-ORDINATES!
-16.286571, -67.795138

WHEN SHOULD I GO?
Ideally sometime before you retire

HOW LONG WILL IT TAKE?
15 hours without toilet breaks

HOW DO I GET THERE?
From Europe it's a long haul to Lima or Bogata before connecting to La Paz

WHAT'S THE WEATHER LIKE?
Sketchy

WHAT'S THE ROAD LIKE?
Sketchier

WHAT IF I GET LOST?
Leave a trail of breadcrumbs and you'll be fine

TG TOP TIP:
Only go over the Guallatiri volcano if you have Viagra. It helps with the altitude…

ONE MORE THING:
This trip starts on the Yungas Road, otherwise known as the Highway of Death. You've been warned

INDEX